WHAT ABOUT TOMORROW?

A Practical Guide
For
The Purposeful Youth

FEMI LAWANI

ISBN 978-0-95565259-1-8

DEDICATION

To the loving and good memory of my father, **Rev. Vincent A. Lawani,** who lived and died in the service of the Most High God and taught me and my siblings the importance of hard work, honesty, integrity and most importantly, the fear of God.
I sincerely know you would have been very proud of me.
Sleep well until the resurrection day.

CONTENTS

ACKNOWLEDGMENTS

I will be forever grateful to the Lord God Almighty for the desire and the abundant grace He has bestowed on me to write this book. The wisdom and ability to see the work to conclusion is appreciated. I can only say Thank You Lord.

I want to thank youths and young people, the world over, whose lives have been touched and positively affected by mine in any way, shape or form. I say a big thank you for allowing me access into your space. I specifically want to appreciate the Youth Excos of LIFE Chapel, Ikorodu, Lagos, for challenging me and bringing out the best in me as Youth President. The inaugural leaders and members of the Teens church of LIFE, for believing in me as a young and the first Teens' pastor are all remembered and appreciated as well. Alex Adegoke, Femi Oboye, Joke, Tinu and Debo Oyelade, Dami and Dorcas Olateru, Toyin And Tayo Oladele, Tobi and Tosin Oluwashina, Bimbo and Shade Oshinbajo, Segun and Gbemi Ogunlusi and many others too numerous to name. We sure did have a lot of fun growing together. Thank You.

I also want to thank Rev. Isaac Olatunde Adeyemi and Rev. (Mrs) Foluke Adeyemi District Overseer, Foursquare Gospel church, Ikorodu 2, for the opportunity to serve in various capacities, the youth and the teenagers then. More grace sir/ma. My sincere appreciation also goes to Rev. Akeem Adeyemi and the entire pioneering members of Kent Foursquare Gospel Church, London for the chance to be of mutual blessings to the youths in the church. You are always on my mind. I appreciate Rev. S.K. Ayanfeola, the General overseer of Comforter Bible Church, Lagos for your encouragement to write this book. Thanks sir. Someone once said 'You will either be a good example or a horrible warning'[1]. Thank you for all that you did for me.

I honestly thank Dr. Wale and Sister Danielle Obe for encouraging and praying for me. Thank you for reading through the initial work and pulling it apart. Big thanks to my brother, Peter Lawani for challenging me to do better with the work. God's blessing be exponentially multiplied unto you.

I really do acknowledge and appreciate Pastor Michael Olawore

---

[1] Catherine Aird. British Novelist And Author

and the leadership of New Wine Church, London for the opportunity given to serve. Bro. Wale Shatimehin is worthy of mention. Thanks.

Let me also mention and appreciate Pastor Bayo and Sister Bola Lawal of Foursquare Gospel Church, Essex for their encouragement. May the work of God in your hands prosper beyond your imagination. Pastor Dare Osatimehin of Total Word Ministries, England, thank you sir for your patience and encouragement. I also recognise and salute Pastor Faith Oluwagbesan of Church Without Bounds, Lagos, you are an inspiration, an epitome of purposeful youthfulness. Thank you.

I will finally want to thank my darling sweetheart, Tayo for your support in every way. Your advice, suggestions and corrections are valuable and appreciated. I do really love and appreciate you. Big shout out to my children, Timi for typing the original manuscript, Dami, Esther and Vicky for giving Daddy the time to do this work. I love you guys to bits.

To all my colleagues, friends and family, who have always believed in God's grace and ability in my life, thank you. May the good Lord make your tomorrow better than your today and make your life a channel of blessing to generations yet unborn in Jesus name.

PREFACE

There is an urgent need for our youths today to understand and appreciate this fact of life; there is a tomorrow. Tomorrow is symbolic of and connotes the future, especially the very near future.'[2]

We all have a future in our timeline, which must be taken care of in the immediate. We have always heard it said that failing to plan is planning to fail. It is alarming, to say the least, at how many young people live their lives without paying the slightest thought to and consciously making any concrete plans for tomorrow.

Successes in life do not just happen, they are planned for. Great academic, marital and spiritual achievements and attainments are by-products of a carefully orchestrated and detailed plan, more than any other thing. You are personally responsible for how your life ultimately turns out. You have no one or anything to blame.

This book is an attempt to encourage, challenge, instruct and practically guide the young person into and through a life of conscious and deliberate planning for Tomorrow. It is set to challenge the status quo in believing that 'Que sera sera' (what will be will be), but to rather imbibe and embrace the notion that if it's going to be, it's up to me! It is to provoke the youth into a holistic comprehension of life with a view to ultimately enjoying it in abundance.

It is borne out of my personal desire to raise purposeful, objective, practical and successful young people through the teaching of the undiluted truth of God's word that is scripturally based and practical in nature.

What About Tomorrow? Is a question that needs to be asked often and it is my sincere belief and expectation, that this book will challenge everyone who intends to succeed in life; to aim higher and live out a more fulfilling life. It is set to build the next generation of territory takers and kingdom expanders. This book is a result of my many years of experience working with youths and young adults as Counselor, Youth President, Youth and Teenagers' Pastor, in different countries.

The book has been carefully broken into four major sections, dealing with what I consider the key foundations to living a fulfilled

---

[2] Oxford Dictionary of Contemporary English

life. Taking a cue from the life of Jacob in the bible, who left his father's house a fugitive, but was wise enough to seek and take God in his journey of life. He discovered his purpose in life, fell in love, married his heartthrob and raised a family, all in a foreign land and then asked the very important question 'when shall I prepare for my own house also?'[3].

I will also be drawing on the experiences of present day men and women, who through the discovery and the relentless pursuit of their God given purpose, have positively impacted lives the world over. I believe that this book will appeal and be of tremendous impact to Youth and Teen leaders, Pastors and young people everywhere who desire to achieve a godly balance in their future.

It is my prayer that as you read this book, the Holy Spirit of God will illuminate your heart and grant you divine wisdom to comprehend the truth herein. You will be able to appropriate and put into action the wisdom imbibed and always ask the question 'What About Tomorrow'?

See you at the top!

'Femi Lawani
London, December 2014

---

[3] Genesis 30:30b

FOREWORD

The total journey of a man's life is summed and wrapped up together in purpose. Purpose is what everyone lives for. The presence of it gives direction and the lack of it makes life miserable.

"For You formed my inward parts; You covered me in my mother's womb. I will praise You, for I am fearfully and wonderfully made; marvellous are Your works, And that my soul knows very well." (Psalms 139:13, 14 NKJV).

If God formed our inward parts, then it will be a good idea if we can also consult with Him so as to be able to determine the step by step model of how to run our lives.

That is why it will not be out of place to find out why you are here and what you are here for. The only one you can inquire from is the one who authored you and this is why I agree with the author of this book that you need a time of spiritual preparation.

Beloved, you are created to project the beauty of your creator. He has a beauty that you must search for to discover and live out. That is your purpose. The Bible says *"...For this purpose the Son of God was manifested, that He might destroy the works of the devi.l"* (1 John 3:8 NKJV).

What is your own purpose for living? Jesus' reason for living was to destroy the works of the devil. Why are you here, what are you here for? These are the questions the author tries to provide answers for and going forward helps us to chart the course to discover and fulfil purpose with dispatch.

Having read through the manuscript, I concluded that this book is a must-read for both young and old who desire to finish gloriously. You are fearfully and wonderfully made to discover, declare and manifest purpose. That is what makes you a celebrity.

Isaac Adeyemi
Host Pastor, FGC Livingspring Tabernacle
Lagos, Nigeria.

CHAPTER 1

SPIRITUAL PREPARATION

Blaise Pascal, a 16th century French mathematician and philosopher, once said, 'there is a God-shaped vacuum in the heart of every person, which cannot be filled by anything, but only by God the creator, made known through Jesus.' People down through the ages have attempted, without any success, to fill this vacuum with things such as drugs, sex, money, beauty, fame, prostitution, occult practices, etc. Someone put it very succinctly that without God, the creator of life, life makes no sense. There is no sense of purpose in and meaning associated with life, without giving God, His rightful place. It is only the manufacturer of a product that can actually determine the full potential of the product. He alone knows what the product is capable of doing and achieving. I want to sincerely presume, that we do not believe any of these evolution theories that say humans are descendants of apes and monkeys.

> *It is only the manufacturer of a product that can actually determine the full potential of the product.*

The evolution theory as propounded by Charles Darwin concludes that apes have evolved over time to become us, human beings. As far as I am concerned, I certainly am not an ape. What about you? The bible says in Genesis 1:1, "*In the beginning God, created the heavens and the earth.*' Genesis 1:26 and 27 say, "*Then God said, 'Let us make human beings in our image, to be like ourselves. They will reign over the fish in the sea, the birds in the sky, the livestock and all the wild animals on the earth, and the small animals that scurry along the ground.' So*

God created human beings in His own image. In the image of God he created them; male and female he created them."

Having established that God is the creator and 'manufacturer' of life, it follows logically that, only He can fully determine the 'true' purpose of life. So for any person, more so a young one, to make a success of life, the first place to start is finding out or discovering their purpose from God. You really cannot determine your purpose, you can only discover it. For each and every one of us there is a purpose for which we have been made and sent into this world. This reminds me of the poem by Russell Kelfer, which goes thus:

> You are who you are for a reason
> You are part of an intricate plan
> You are a precious and perfect unique design
> Called God's special woman/man.
>
> You look how you look for a reason
> Our God made no mistake
> He knit you together within the womb
> You're just what he wanted.
>
> The parents you have are the ones he chose
> And no matter how you feel
> They were customed, designed, with God's plan in mind
> And they bear the master's seal.
>
> No, the trauma you faced was not easy
> And God wept that it hurt you so
> But it was allowed to shape your heart
> So that into his likeness you'd grow.
>
> You are who you are for a reason
> You've been formed by the master's rod
> You are who you are beloved
> Because there is a God.

Therefore it follows logic to start our lifelong preparation with a definite encounter with God, the creator of life.

There are three aspects of spiritual preparation that every

aspiring young person should deliberately pursue. Everyone born into this world comes into what I call 'a well-rehearsed theatre of sins and iniquities with many years of experience behind it'. This means that the world that we find ourselves in, is full of sinful habits that have been in continual practice and improvement for upward of six millenniums. From the moment you are born, you inherit that nature of sin and until you deliberately decide to do something about it, you just go on wallowing in sins all the days of your live.

You came with a body, a soul, and a spirit. Unfortunately your spirit at birth is dead to God and righteousness, and your soul, which is the seat of emotions and will, is only tending and gravitating towards evil continually. Genesis 6:5 says, *"And God saw that the wickedness of man was great in the earth, and that every imagination of the thoughts of his heart was only evil continually."* Jeremiah 17:9 says, *"The heart is deceitful above all things, and desperately wicked: who can know it?"* Our decision to establish a connection with God our maker, can only be done through the transformation and resuscitation of our spirit. This is why we must begin with spiritual preparation in our quest to find a purpose and make a success of our lives.

Let us carefully look at these areas with a view to understanding the steps to take:

1. DISCOVER YOUR PURPOSE

We have agreed earlier that no man/product can determine his purpose, we can only discover it. The major difference between a highly successful and thriving individual and a struggling one, is that the former has discovered his purpose for life, while the latter has not. For the avoidance of doubt, what exactly is purpose? It is defined by the Oxford English Dictionary as 'the reason for which something is or created, or for which something exists.' This means for anyone to succeed or triumph in the race of life, he/she must find out the reason for which he/she has been created.

There are many people in life who do not have a clue as to the reason why they are alive. Some people some time ago said, 'Let us eat and drink; for tomorrow, we die.'[4] No sense of direction. Nothing to achieve, other than to live today and die tomorrow. The highway of life is strewn with carcasses of people who have lived and died without having discovered the reason for which they were created. I have met people in my time who live their lives without any sense of direction. Young people with plenty of potential to succeed and excel have not attained to those prospects, simply because they did not find out why they are here.

There are many books on purpose out there, but multiplied millions of young people have failed, albeit, unintentionally to take advantage of them. This book in your hand, amongst other things, is to challenge you to take time out to find out what your purpose on earth is. Pastor Seye Awopetu, in his book, Created For A Purpose, says, 'Discovering God's purpose therefore means your attempt to understand what God has in His mind when He conceived the idea of creating you'. Jeremiah 1:5 says, *"I knew you before I formed you in your mother's womb. Before you were born I set you apart and appointed you as my prophet to the nations."* (NLT).

Mark Zuckerberg, the chairman and chief executive of Facebook, inc, a multi-billion dollar company, at the age of 30 years, said in January 2014 in an interview, 'I remember really vividly, you know, having pizza with my friends a day or two after I opened up the first version of Facebook, at the time I thought, 'You know, someone needs to build a service like this for the world.' But I just never thought that we'd be the ones to help do it. And I think a lot of what it comes down to is we just cared more'[5]. Can we just imagine what the world would have been like without the social networking site? As at 2012, Mark Zuckerberg, was voted the 2nd youngest self- made billionaire[6], edged out only by Dustin Moskovitz, also a co-founder of Facebook. He is worth a staggering $33.1 billion as at July 2014[7]. I believe the world is waiting for your own discovery and innovation, which will be of

---

[4] Isaiah 22:13

[5] Jason Fell (14 may 2014). 'As mark Zuckerberg Turns 30, His 10 Best Quotes As CEO'

[6] Forbes's Youngest Billionaire: Retrieved 29/12/2012

[7] 'Mark Zuckerberg'. Forbes

great benefit to all mankind. Do not delay. The earlier you discover
your reason for existence, the better your chances of success. Set
out on a personal discovery adventure to find out your purpose.
Two major questions to ask yourself in the pursuit of the discovery
of your purpose are:

WHO AM I? and WHAT AM I DOING HERE?

For everyone who has ever attained anything of notable
significance, these two questions have been asked and satisfactorily
answered.

I am reminded of the story of a depressed Rabbi during the
Russian occupation and oppression of his land and people. He was
so despondent and confused that he wandered into a military
camp, where he was startled with a shout of command by the guard
who said, 'Who are you and what are you doing here?'

The depressed Rabbi snapped out of his despondency and
asked the soldier, 'How much are you getting paid doing this job?'

'About $25 a month,' the guard answered.

'I will pay you twice that amount if you continue to ask me
those two questions every day."

We need to ask ourselves these two questions on a daily basis.
The first one deals with our identity and the second deals with our
reason for existence. You must know for sure who you really are. If
you don't know who you are it will be virtually impossible to fully
maximize your potential. So the billion dollar question is: Who are
you?

WHO AM I?

There has been a misunderstanding of this question over the
centuries. From the time of Adam in the Bible up to this age and
time, people have misunderstood this question and consequently
incorrectly answered it. In Genesis 3:9-11, "*the LORD God called
unto Adam, and said unto him, Where are you?*

*10 And he said, I heard your voice in the garden, and I was afraid,
because I was naked; and I hid myself.*

*11 And he said, who told you that you were naked? Have you eaten of the
tree, of which I commanded you that you should not eat?*"

Many people have mistaken their position, status, gender and
titles to define who they are. You will be shocked at how many
Christians will feel disrespected if you do not add their titles and

educational prefix when they are being introduced. There was a story of an invited guest minister in a church who refused to actually get up and preach because the announcer did not call him by his 'full title' (Rev. Dr. Eng., etc). You might say piously, 'that is ridiculous,' or 'I will never do that,' but trust me, it takes someone who really knows their true identity in Christ and secured in that knowledge not to be bothered. So the question is, 'who are you?'

Stop right now and ponder over that question for a while and write down the first five things that pop into mind. Chances are you write things like these:

I am a man/woman   male/female

I am a student/doctor/businessman

I am married with ...... number of children.

I am called.......

I am from.........

In stark contrast to who we think we are, it is actually advisable to go and discover from the manufacturer's manual of life, who we truly are. What does your maker say about you? Go through the manual (the Bible) to find out what your maker says about you. Remember, only He, as your manufacturer, can correctly decide and decipher your potentials. God said in 1Peter 2:9-10, *"But you are a chosen generation, a royal priesthood, a holy nation, His own special people, that you may proclaim the praise of Him who called you out of darkness into His marvelous light."*

Matthew 16:13-17 talks about a conversation Jesus had with his disciples, where the question of his identity was discussed.

13 "When Jesus came into the region of Caesarea Philippi, He asked His disciples, saying, 'who do men say that I, the son of Man, am?'

14 So they said, 'Some say John the Baptist, some Elijah, and others Jeremiah or one of the prophets'

15 He said to them, 'But who do you say that I am?'

16 Simon Peter answered and said, 'You are the Christ, the son of the living God.'

17 Jesus answered and said to him, 'Blessed are you, Simon Bar-Jonah, for flesh and blood has not revealed this to you, but My father who is in heaven."

Also in John 10:10, Jesus said. *"The thief does not come except to steal, and to kill, and to destroy. I have come that they may have life, and that they may have it more abundantly."*

Jesus furthermore declared in Luke 4:18-19, *"The spirit of the*

Lord is upon me, Because He has anointed me to preach the gospel to the poor; He has sent me to heal the broken-hearted, And recovery of sight to the blind, To set at liberty those who are oppressed;

19 To proclaim the acceptable year of the Lord."

These passages show without any ambiguity who Jesus was and the purpose of His coming to the earth. No wonder he could fulfil those without being distracted. So the question is who are You?

My father of blessed memory, was someone who I personally have a lot of respect for in this regard. He was approached many times during his life time to start a church and/or Ministry. He usually responded by saying that God has not called him to start a church, but to build Christian leaders through sound teachings. He did that with all sense of duty, rising to become the Director of Christian Education of a very well established denomination in his country before his death.[8]

WHAT AM I DOING HERE?

The second question that helps you determine your purpose in life is, 'What am I doing here?' We need to constantly ask ourselves this question to help us keep focused on what is our primary assignment on earth. Everyone that is born into this world has an assignment to undertake. We have been commissioned by our maker to fulfil a certain purpose here on earth. Whether we now live to fulfil that is a different kettle of fish altogether. Les Brown, an American motivational speaker and author of worship books said, 'The graveyard is the richest place on earth, because it is here you will find all the hopes and dreams that were never fulfilled, the books that were never written, the songs that were never sung, the inventions that were never shared, the cures that were never discovered, all because someone was too afraid to take that first step, keep with the problem, or determined to carry out their dreams.'[9] Permit me to

> *We have been commissioned by our maker to fulfil a certain purpose here on earth.*

---

[8] In His Service. A Biography of Rev. Vincent Lawani. 2012
[9] Live Your Dreams. Les Brown

add that buried there are people who have died without fulfilling their full potentials on earth.

There in the cemeteries lie great medical and scientific discoveries that will never be made, powerful messages and sermons that will never be preached, life touching and melodious songs that will never be heard, great corporations that will never be formed and many more. I decree and declare that you will fulfil your destiny/purpose in Jesus' name. Myles Munroe talks about 'Dying Empty' which means doing all that God has put in you before you die. The first place to achieve this is by discovering the exact reason for your present existence. You are not just an accident of history or mere statistics in the government database. You really do matter to God.

Two quick reasons why you must find out your purpose on earth and fulfil it are:

1. You have the unquantifiable joy and pleasure of accomplishing your God assigned purpose and at the end of your life's journey you can say like Apostle Paul in 2 Timothy 4:7, *"I have fought a good fight, I have finished my course, and I have kept the faith..."* What a sense of accomplishment.

2. Secondly, your discovery and dogged pursuit of your reason for living will help others to quickly achieve their own purpose and assignment. This presupposes that there are other people's destinies that are tied to your success or otherwise. For every young person who fails to achieve their God ordained purpose, there are lives in multiples that will be negatively affected. So it is not just about you, it is about multiple futures that will be affected by your action or inaction.

A close look at the lives of people like Steve Jobs, the co-founder, chairman and CEO of Apple Inc. whose ingenuity and innovations has made the company rake in billions in revenue and even in death, the company, Apple Inc. is one of the richest companies in the world with a revenue of $170billion and a total number of 80,300 employees worldwide.[10]

Facebook Inc., co-founded by Mark Zuckerberg at the age of 20 in 2004, is worth over $55billion,[11] employs close to 8,000 staff and is being used by 1.32 billion people as at June 2014. Microsoft

---

[10] List of Largest Companies by Revenue, 2014
[11] Celebrity Networth, Top 50 Companies 2014

Corporation, founded by Bill Gates in 1975, has a revenue in excess of $86 billion in 2014 and employs over 128,000 people as at June 2014.[12]

People like Michael Jackson, Nelson Rohilala Mandela, Warren Buffet and many more have made significant impact in our days because they knew why they were alive and vigorously pursued that course. We are all touched in one way or another by their influence in our lives.

The book of Hebrews 12:1 says, *"Therefore, since we are surrounded by such a great cloud of witnesses, let us throw off everything that hinders and the sins that so easily entangles, and let us run with perseverance the race marked out for us."*

I pray for you right now that you will not disappoint your generation. Generations yet unborn will thank God that you lived and fulfilled your assignment. I presently live in England from where I run my business. I am privileged to travel fairly often and meet many people from my country of origin. I get to introduce myself quite a lot too. The interesting thing is that I have never met anyone who has anything bad to say about my biological father. I cannot count how many people have helped me just because they know or have heard about my father. That has always been a source of encouragement and challenge to me to always positively influence people.

In Romans 5:19, the Bible talks about the generational impact of disobedience and obedience. The Bible says, *"For just as through the disobedience of one man, many were made sinners, so also through the obedience of the one man, many will be made righteous."* What does that really mean? It means that through the disobedience and rebellion of one man, Adam, we all became sinners down through the ages. As a result of Adam and Eve's disobedience, we became enemies of God, cut off from true fellowship and union with our maker. We became conceived in sin and birthed in iniquities. However, through the obedience of Jesus Christ to die on the cross, we were reconciled with God. We that were not a people, have now through faith in Christ's finished work, become THE people of God.

---

[12] Wikipedia: Microsoft Corporation

We can deduce that when Adam and Eve disobeyed God, you and I were not there, but we partook of the consequences. So also when Christ was obeying God to the point of death on the cross, we were also not there, but today we enjoy the benefits therein. The question to you now, is what choices are you making now that will affect not only you, but your unborn generations? Think and choose carefully.

> *What choices are you making now that will affect not only you, but your unborn generations?*

The most important step in our spiritual preparation, after acknowledging our state of hopelessness in sin and in need for God's help of salvation, is to discover our purpose on earth. Know who you are and what you have been assigned to do and make up your mind never to die until you achieve it.

2. CUT A DEAL WTH GOD

As a businessman of long standing, I am always negotiating and making deals. I have come to discover that the God we serve is a principled God. Being principled means you have a set of rules and regulations that you follow fastidiously. You do not practice double standard. The God of the Bible is actually the simplest and most straightforward being there is. He tells you beforehand what He requires from you and the consequences of breaking these rules as exemplified in His Transactional dealings with His people in the Old Testament. If you take a good look at Deuteronomy 28, you will understand that dealing with God is very easy, for as long as you stay true to your agreement, you are fine. But the moment you break the deal, you will pay the price.

This has been described by bible scholars as the view of God that leads to 'legalism and performance based'. We are now under a better covenant of grace, which has the relational view of God as our loving heavenly father, who, because of the death and resurrection of Jesus, is more than willing to give us all that pertains to live and godliness.

Cutting a deal with God, in this context, means that as a young person, you have a personal encounter with God and enter into an agreement with Him. Sign a memorandum of understanding with God. Go through his 'manual' and verbally commit yourself to Him. Tell him what you want Him to do and what you will do in return. Let us look at an example of that in Genesis 28:10-22.

"10 And Jacob went out from Beersheba, and went toward Haran.

11 And he came upon a certain place, and tarried there all night, because the sun was set; and he took of the stones of that place, and put them for his pillows, and lay down in that place to sleep.

12 And he dreamed, and behold a ladder set up on the earth, and the top of it reached to heaven: and behold the angels of God ascending and descending on it.

13 And, behold, the LORD stood above it, and said, I am the LORD God of Abraham your father, and the God of Isaac: the land on which you lie, to you will I give it, and to your descendants;

14 And your descendants shall be as the dust of the earth, and you shall spread abroad to the west, and to the east, and to the north, and to the south: and in you and in your descendants shall all the families of the earth be blessed.

15 And, behold, I am with you, and will keep you in all places wherever you go, and will bring you again into this land; for I will not leave you, until I have done that which I have spoken to you of.

16 And Jacob awaked out of his sleep, and he said, Surely the LORD is in this place; and I knew it not.

17 And he was afraid, and said, How dreadful is this place! this is none other but the house of God, and this is the gate of heaven.

18 And Jacob rose up early in the morning, and took the stone that he had put for his pillows, and set it up for a pillar, and poured oil upon the top of it.

19 And he called the name of that place Bethel: but the name of that city was called Luz at first.

20 And Jacob vowed a vow, saying, If God will be with me, and will keep me in this way that I go, and will give me bread to eat, and clothing to put on,

21 So that I come again to my father's house in peace; then shall the LORD be my God:

22 And this stone, which I have set for a pillar, shall be God's house: and of all that you shall give me I will surely give the tenth unto you."

This was an account of a young man named Jacob, who had just cheated his elder brother of his birth-right blessings and was running away from his home for dear life. He got to a certain place and being wearied of the journey, decided to pass the night there.

He had a dream and saw the Lord telling him what He would do for him on this journey of his. When he arose the next day, from verse 20, he made a vow unto God to build God's house, using the stone he set up as the pillar and to give God a tenth of all that God gave him. God is a covenant keeping God. He is not a man who would lie nor the son of man that He should repent[13]. When He says a thing, He does it. He blessed Jacob in a foreign land as agreed and later on in Genesis 35:1-3, you will also see the fulfilment of Jacob's vow to God.

"Then God said to Jacob, "Arise, go up to Bethel and live there, and make an altar there to God, who appeared to you when you fled from your brother Esau." 2So Jacob said to his household and to all who were with him, "Put away the foreign gods which are among you, and purify yourselves and change your garments; 3and let us arise and go up to Bethel, and I will make an altar there to God, who answered me in the day of my distress and has been with me wherever I have gone."

The lesson we learn here is this: for your spiritual journey in life, you must above other things do the following;

Have God In And With You Always

Your strength can only carry you thus far. You need God to be on your side. It is often said that one with God is a majority. Ezra Taft Benson, said, 'When you kneel before God, you will stand before anyone.' Too many people set out, often with catastrophic consequences, without God. They just assume that life will play out and things will work out. Young people, please take all the time in the world to get it right with God. I am not talking of being religious here. I am saying, develop a very personal and intimate relationship with your maker. Many of us are born into Christian homes, we have been going to church all our lives. We have fanciful Christian names and we just assume that we know God. I had to personally, on the 7th

> *Too many people set out, often with catastrophic consequences, without God.*

---

[13] Numbers 23:19 (KJV)

of January, 1990 give my life to Christ in a service and I can say that God has been good to me since then. It is ludicrous to believe that you will make it without your manufacturer.

I was watching the result of the autopsy on the famous singer, Whitney Huston the other day, and I realized that she died of drug overdose. Someone who started singing in the church choir at a very young age lost her way because she did not personally know the God of the church as typified by her way of life, which included drug addiction and abuse.

Determine To Serve God Whole Heartedly

There are no half measures with God. You are either all in or not in at all. It is either you want to serve God with your whole life or not. There is no sitting on the fence. No one leg in and one leg out business. Totally commit to him. Make Him Lord of all or He is not Lord at all. Determine to make Him famous through all your actions. Deliberately decide to be sold out to Him and His cause and you will never miss your place in life. I remember when I was leaving for England years back; I determined to serve God in the foreign land. I remember entering an agreement with God that I will not get involved in anything that will bring shame to His name in return for Him guiding and making my sojourn in the land fruitful and worthwhile. There were a lot of temptations to use shortcuts to achieve financial breakthrough which I had to fight almost on a daily basis. God eventually came through for me according to His promises and settled me in a very short time in the land. I actually did everything I set out to achieve and much more.

There was a time when I looked back and said to a friend of mine that I have achieved everything I wanted in England. This book and others to come, and many other spiritual exploits are partial fulfilments of my part of the deal.

Know And Follow God Wholeheartedly

There is something as knowing God. God can and will be known if you seek Him with the whole of your heart. Jeremiah 29:13 says, *"And you will seek Me and find Me, when you search for Me with all your heart."*

Knowing God starts with having a working knowledge and understanding of His personality. What does He want and like? What are his preferences and desires? I am always intrigued and totally confused when people say you cannot know God. All you need to know about God is in His constitution/manual. If I want to know what a country is like in terms of laws and compositions, I only need to start by consulting the constitution of that country. Read and find out what constitutes a violation of their laws and the penalties attached to them.

Many Christians are lazy to even find out what their Holy Book says about different issues of life. They do not always know what God wants in regards to their health, successes, relationships, etc. If you want to make a success of your life, take time out to really 'know God'. Take His word and read it until it stops being just a written word (Logos) but becomes life (Rhema). Let it minister to you so much that you cannot be fooled or tossed by any wind of fake doctrines. Our generation and those coming behind will witness an unprecedented and deliberate presentation of falsehood by various media. Only those who are grounded in the true word of God will be able to differentiate the lies from the truth. The following steps are recommended:

1. Give your life to Christ genuinely and totally.

2. Follow a systematic and fun filled way of reading the Bible consistently every day, such as phones, iPad, Electronic tablet, Mp3, etc.

3. Attach yourself to a bible preaching and believing church where you will be fed with the undiluted truth of God's word. Be conscious of what theologians call 'heresy', which is not just preaching outright lies, but also magnifying one truth as absolute over others.

4. Develop a consistent walk with God by listening to His voice for direction over all issues in your life. Let the Holy Spirit continue to guide you into what is right and keep you from what is wrong. I cannot overemphasize the importance of this as a young person.

Having known God, you need to make up your mind to follow Him wholeheartedly. Serving God wholeheartedly is putting him first in all areas. Let His business become paramount to you. If you take care of God's business from your early years, God will not leave your own business unattended. You will not lose your place in life. Prophet Samuel in the Bible is a good example. He was consecrated unto God from childhood and for a period spanning 40 years, as ruler of God's people, enjoyed God's blessings. 1 Samuel 3:19 says, *"And Samuel grew, and the LORD was with him, and did let none of his words fall to the ground."*

We have genuine ministers of God in our days who follow God wholeheartedly and God has honoured them greatly. Add your name to the growing lists of Apostles and Generals of God in this age. I am of the opinion that the 'Acts of Apostles' of Christ which can also be said to be the Acts of Jesus Christ by the Apostles, through the Holy Spirit is continuous and ongoing. It did not end with Paul and others and your name and mine can and should be added to the lists of exploits done.

I therefore challenge you to be prepared spiritually for the world out there. You need inner fortification by the almighty God to help you through life. Everything that happens in the physical realm is first concluded in the spiritual realm. The spiritual actually controls the physical. It therefore follows that to succeed in the physical world, we must have the backing of the spiritual. Get connected to the ultimate source of spiritual power. I dare you to discover your purpose for life, cut a deal with God and strive to know and follow God wholeheartedly.

> *If you take care of God's business from your early years, God will not leave your own business unattended.*

See you at the top!

CHAPTER 2

EDUCATIONAL PREPARATION

'Education is the most powerful weapon which you can use to change the world.'
-Nelson Mandela

The importance of educational preparation for a 'successful' life cannot be over emphasized. The 21st century youth cannot afford to be uneducated. The world we live in is fast evolving. Knowledge is vastly available now more than at any other time in human history. The spread of information through various media is unprecedented and is not about to stop.

Education is the process of learning and Knowing, which is not restricted to our school text books. It is a holistic process and continues through our life. Even the regular happenings and events around us educate us, in one way or another. It would not be an exaggeration to say that the existence of human beings is fruitless without education. An educated person is brimming with confidence and assured of making the right moves. 'The purpose of education is to replace an empty mind with an open one.'[14]

Young people are acquiring greater educational and academic levels more quickly than at any other time in the past. It is common to see boys and girls in their early twenties with more than one or two academic qualifications. It is therefore pathetic and almost inconceivable why young people even in developed countries such as the United Kingdom and the United States are not interested in education.

According to a publication of the UK Parliament of the 21st of August, 2014, around 955,000 people aged 16-24 were classified as

---

[14] Malcolm Forbes – Publisher, Forbes Magazine

Not in Education, Employment or Training (NEET) in the second quarter of 2014[15]. In Japan, the figure was put at 850,000 for people between the ages of 25-34.[16]

In Canada the figure is 904,000 as at 2013 for youth between the ages of 15-29.[17] This figure gets worse in countries such as Niger and Pakistan, where more than two of every three young people are Not in Education, Employment or Training.[18]

Malcolm X puts it accurately when he said, 'Without education, you are not going anywhere in this world.'[19]

I will never forget ministering to young people in Birmingham, a town in England, where almost half the participants are not in school or employment. When I asked why that was so, I heard excuses such as, "I'm just not interested,' and 'You don't need college/university degrees to make money in life.' Really? Mary J. Blige said, 'I wish I had known that education is key. That knowledge is power. Now I pick up books and watch educational shows with my husband. I'm seeing how knowledge can elevate you.'[20] Phil Mickelson reiterated this when he submitted that, 'I think a college education is important no matter what you do in life.'[21]

> *There is no mountain anywhere; everyone's ignorance is their own mountain*

Education is that which transforms a person to live a better life and even in a social well-being. Education helps us do something constructive with our near future (tomorrow). It gives you a lot of knowledge in different aspects and by God you cannot afford to be ignorant in this age and in your tomorrow. Bishop David Oyedepo once said, 'There is no mountain anywhere; everyone's ignorance is their own

---

[15] House Of Commons Standard Note. SN/EP/06705
[16] The Asia-pacific Journal: Japan Focus, 2014
[17] Statistics Canada, October, 2014
[18] Wikipedia, The Free Encyclopedia
[19] Malcolm X – Black American Human Right Activist. (1925-1965)
[20] Mary J. Blige - American singer, Song Writer and Actress
[21] Phil Mickelson - American Professional Golfer

mountain.'[22] Education plays a vital role in your success in the personal growth. The more you know, the more you grow. The day you stop learning is the day you start dying, at least intellectually. Being educated and earning a professional degree set you apart in reputed organizations, companies and institution. For determining what is good or what is bad for you, education will help you. 'Education is the power to think clearly, the power to act well in the worlds work, and the power to appreciate life.'[23]

In today's competitive world, education is necessity for people after food, clothing and shelter. While education might not be the solution to every problem, it promotes good habits, values and awareness towards anything like terrorism, corruption, and much more. Simply put education is the backbone of everyone's life as said by Plato, 'If a man neglects education, he walks lame to the end of his life.'[24]

7 EXTREMELY IMPORTANT REASONS TO BE EDUCATED

1. EDUCATION HELPS YOU TO BUILD A CAREER

To build a successful career in any field of human endeavour, you need good education. Education gives you the knowledge of your field so that you can pursue the career of your interest fully fledged. On the contrary, those who are illiterate are considered for labour/manual jobs which do not require understanding, knowledge or development. They act as a source to the needs of the educated. Hence, to have a secure and balanced career, we need to work hard, learn new things, gain knowledge, spread our experience and help the society. Bill Gates said, 'Unemployment rates among Americans who never went to college are about double that of those who have a postsecondary education.'[25]

---

[22] Bishop David Oyedepo – Founder and Presiding Bishop, Living Faith World Wide

[23] Brigham Young – 2nd President, Latter Day Saint Movement

[24] Plato – Philosopher And Mathematician, Ancient Greece

[25] Bill Gates. Founder, Microsoft Corporations

2. EDUCATION PROVIDES WISDOM

Education is often compared with wisdom. A person who is educated has both knowledge and wisdom. Wisdom to know the correct thing to do and knowledge to reason it. Wisdom acts as the stepping stone during a person's growth. A lot of these can be taught to you in schools/colleges. Education also gives you a sense of right and wrong. To know if you are right, you must know what is right. 'Knowledge is power. Information is liberating. Education is the premise of progress, in every society, in every family.'[26] If we go by the terms of what people say, there will be a huge confusion in our understanding, leading us to unwanted and dodgy situations. This can only be corrected or checked if we are educated enough not to be waved away. 2 Timothy 2:15 says, *"study to show thy self approved unto God, a workman that needeth not to be ashamed, rightly dividing the word of truth."*

3. EDUCATION PROVIDES KNOWLEDGE

'The goal of education is the advancement of knowledge and the dissemination of truth.'[27] Education makes you knowledgeable. It makes you stand tall in a discussion and participate enthusiastically with no shame of going dumb. Knowledge makes you aware, potentially updated and open minded. A person who lacks knowledge is considered to be foolish and is regarded as either a learner or an illiterate. Hosea 4:6 says, *"My people perish because of lack of knowledge."* Thomas Henry Haxley, a 19th century English Biologist said, 'Try to learn everything about something and something about everything.'

> *Try to learn everything about something and something about everything.*

4. EDUCATION PROVIDES INDEPENDENCE

---

[26] Kofi Annan – Former Secretary General, United Nations
[27] John F. Kennedy, 35th American President. (1917-1963)

Education makes our growth optimism and helps you become independent to start your own life. It makes you reliable on your instincts and knowledge to take the right decision that does not harm your image and respect. An independent thought process is developed when your brain is open to all the forms of life and knowledge about how advanced the world has become. This makes you create your own mentality rather than being a herd follower of your ancestors and it gives you a broader outlook towards life in general. For instance, how many Christians, old or young, can have an intellectual discourse about the superiority of the Christian faith over other religions or why they believe in Christ for salvation? Just thinking aloud.

5. EDUCATION ENSURES A PRODUCTIVE FUTURE

'Education is the key to the future: You've heard it a million times, and it's not wrong. Educated people have higher wages and lower unemployment rates, and better educated countries grow faster and innovate more than other countries.'[28] Our productivity is increased by acquiring new skills and talents through education. We find ourselves in the most competitive jobs, courtesy of the right training and education. 'A human being is not attaining his full heights until he is educated.'[29]

6. EDUCATION OPENS NEW VISTAS

The significance of education, for a great part, lies in its ability to open new vistas for us. It expands our outlook and teaches us to be tolerant towards other views. 'It is the mark of an educated mind to be able to entertain a thought without accepting it.'[30] An educated person will find it easier to understand a different point of

> *It is the mark of an educated mind to be able to entertain a thought without accepting it.*

---

[28] Alex Tabarrock, Canadian-American Economist
[29] Horace Mann, American Education Reformer and Politician
[30] Aristotle, Greek Philosopher And Scientist

view than the one who is uneducated. Education broadens our mental landscape and is the way forward to greater enlightenment – the ultimate goal to every human in life.

7. EDUCATION SPREADS AWARENESS AND BOLSTERS CONFIDENCE

Awareness is a virtue, the lack of which is lamented everywhere. Education spreads awareness, informing us about our rights and the services we can access. On the most basic notes, it teaches us to differentiate between right and wrong. For most parts of our lives, we falter in deciding between right and wrong, but the right education gives the right answers. An educated person is also a confident person. 'Education is the ability to listen to almost anything without losing your temper or self-confidence.'[31] Education fosters a positive outlook and allows us to believe in ourselves. Self-belief is one of the most wanted traits in a human being and education leads us towards relying on ourselves, making us believe that we can take on the world.

MODES OF EDUCATION

Having looked at the importance of education, let us examine the different modes of education. 'There is no end to education. It is not that you read a book, pass an examination, and finish with education. The whole of life, from the moment you are born to the moment you die, is a process of learning.'[32]

Education in its all-inclusive form goes beyond what takes place within the four walls of the classroom. Education can be attained from outside the school as well as from inside. It has been said that, 'The illiterate of the future will not be the person who cannot read and write, but those cannot learn, unlearn and relearn'[33]

Three modes or what we call types of education exist which are: Formal, Informal and Non-Formal.

---

[31] Robert frost, American Poet
[32] Jiddu Krishnamurti –Indian Speaker,Writer And Philosopher
[33] Alvin Toffler – American Writer And Futurist

A) FORMAL EDUCATION

Education is formal if it has the following characteristics:

I) Planned with a particular end in view. It is given in schools, colleges, universities and other institutions which are established with purpose. In this way it is direct by schooling, instruction, and tuition.

II) Limited to a specific period. Formal education is limited to a specific period or stage. It is provided according to certain set rules and regulations. It is in the form of systematic, planned, and instruction.

III) It has a well defined and systematic curriculum. This curriculum is based on certain aims and objectives. These aims are in conformity with the needs of the society and the state.

IV) Observes strict discipline. Formal education observes strict discipline. The pupil and the teacher are both aware of this fact and we can safely conclude therefore, that any process of teaching which involves supervision, instruction, set plan, definite aims and principle amounts to formal education.

B) INFORMAL EDUCATION

Education is said to be informal if it has the following attributes:

I) Incidental and spontaneous. Informal education is incidental and spontaneous. There is no conscious effort involved in it. The type of teaching taught and learnt in a setting that is formal can be said to be informal. For instance, simple courtesies like 'thank you and please' which are not part of any curriculum are said to be informal teaching. I have met many youths in my lifetime who are not only stupid, but plainly rude. This has nothing to do with how much formal education they have or have not acquired. Let us as parents and responsible adults deliberately teach the next generation the timeless values of: honesty, hard work and the fear of God which unfortunately is not mentioned in school curriculums.

II) Not pre-planned nor deliberate. Informal education is an educative activity which is neither pre-planned nor deliberate. We learn many habits, manners and patterns while living with others or moving in different spheres, like home, society, church groups, etc.

III) Not imparted by any specialized agency. Unlike formal education, informal education is not imparted by any specialized agency such as schools or colleges. There is an African proverb that says, 'Only two people bring a child to the world, but thousands of people bring the child up.'

IV) No prescribed time table or curriculum. There is no set curriculum required. It consists in experiences and actual living in the family or community.

In summary, informal education is the process by which a person imbibes attitudes, develops skills, cultivates values and acquires knowledge without there being any organisation or system about it. This would include the deliberate attempts of parents and elders in the family and community to help the young ones grow and adapt themselves to the environment. Informal education would also include all incidental learning that takes place while at work or at play and during travels as well as spontaneous learning through films, radio and television, e.g., how to prepare a meal.

C) NON-FORMAL EDUCATION

Unlike informal education, which is unstructured, spontaneous and without formality, non-formal education would be structured and planned but outside the realm of formal education. It is any organised, systematic education activity, carried outside the framework of the established formal system whether operating separately or as an important feature of some broad activity that is intended to serve identifiable learning clienteles and learning objectives. This includes Adult Basic Education, Adult Literary Education, Distance Learning, Home Education and Computed-Assisted Instructions.

I have gone to this length to let us understand that there is no tenable excuse for being uneducated and thereby ignorant. We can achieve education in many ways. The 21st century youth cannot afford to be uniformed. We must strive to pursue knowledge at all cost. The bible says, *"Buy the truth and do not sell it..."*

WORLD LEADERS AND EDUCATION

It has often been said, 'Today a reader, tomorrow a leader.' One of the most noticeable trends on the world leaders is that they are almost always without exemption, educated fellows. Countries which excel in both economic and military powers were and are being led by educated men and women.

Most presidents of the United States received a college/university education, even most of the earliest. Of the first seven presidents, five were university/college graduates. Of the 43 men to have been president, 24 of them graduated from a private undergraduate college, nine from a public undergraduate college. Every president from 1869 has had a degree.[34]

In the United Kingdom, of the 54 Prime Ministers to date, 41 of them had a university degree from either Oxford or Cambridge Universities, 3 went to other universities, and so in total 44 of the last 54 Prime Ministers had a university education.[35]

Almost all Canadian Prime Ministers to date, with the exemption of 2 or 3, have at least a university degree, with some who have 2 or 3 additional degrees. The same is true for all of the 7 or 8 most industrialised nations of the world.[36]

It is a gross understatement to say that formal education has lifted and sustained many of these leaders and their countries. Compare these with many third world countries and the difference is crystal clear.

PARADIGM SHIFT

I will want to use this medium to challenge the minority ethnic youths in all these countries to strive for excellence in education. It is not just enough to go to secondary schools and colleges; you must determine to make it to universities and higher colleges for you to be taken seriously. If the above statistics are anything to go by, then the black youths especially, are in the minority in the scheme of things. Leaders, Pastors, Community Elders and Parents must all come together to encourage the next generation of black

---

[34] Wikipedia, List Of American Presidents By Education
[35] Wikispooks, British Prime Ministers
[36] Wikipedia, List Of Prime Ministers of Canada by Academic Degrees

and ethnic minority to attain higher heights in education. Angela Davis once said, 'Poor people, people of colour-especially are much more likely to be found in prison than in institutions of higher education.'[37] We must help our young ones to apply and challenge for places at the top prestigious universities. In 2011 for instance, Oxford University said it accepted only 32 black students which was the highest number they had accepted in 10 years and that white pupils were twice as likely as black pupils to score 3 A*'s at A-Levels.[38]

Did you know that of all the 650 Members of Parliament (MPs) in the House of Commons, who make the laws of the United Kingdom, there are only 27 from the Minority Ethnic Group and only 9 are black?[39] And the report says if the non-white population were represented proportionally in the House of Commons, there would be around 84 Minority ethnic MPs.

In 2013, Rev. Jesse Jackson decries the absence of black students in both Cambridge and Oxford Universities which he said diminishes the greatness of these schools.[40]

I encourage all stakeholders to please ensure that the next generations of young people do not end up as cleaners, bin men/women, train divers, security guards and cabbies, when they can be MPs, surgeons, scientists, lawyers, economists and preachers of the gospel. 'Without education, your children can never really meet the challenges they will face. So it's very important to give children education and explain that they should play a role for their country.'[41]

I think it is high time parents stopped jeopardising and mortgaging the future of their children on the altar of immediate satisfaction of their whims and caprices. I am aware of parents, even Christians, who will rather buy the latest fashion items and attend parties on end, instead of investing in their children's education and future. Barack Hussein Obama, said, 'It's not enough to train today's workforce. We also have to prepare tomorrow's workforce by guaranteeing every child access to a

[37] Angela Davis, American Political Activist
[38] Oxford University
[39] Ethnic Minority in Politics, Government and Public Life. SN/SG/1156, 2013
[40] The Guardian Newspaper, 04/12/2013
[41] Nelson Mandela – 1st Black President Of South Africa

world-class education.'[42] This is gross injustice to the next generation as the bible says, *"A good man leaves an inheritance for his children's children."*[43] Let us think about the kind of legacy we are leaving for our children.

For the youths, it is time to wake up from your slumber and desire a better future for yourself. The one that will make us better off than our parents. If your parents lived all their lives in a council estate, you must aspire to buy your own properties as early as possible. You must not start where your progenitors started. Your tomorrow must be better than your today. You cannot afford to wait a day longer, for the battle of tomorrow has started. You cannot be left behind. Your glorious future beckons and the preparation starts today. 'You must get an education. You must go to school, and you must learn to protect yourself. And you must learn to protect yourself with the pen, and not the gun.'[44]

See you at the top!

---

[42] Barack Obama – 44th President Of The United States of America
[43] Proverbs 13:22 (KJV)
[44] Josephine Baker, American-born French Dancer, Singer and Actress

CHAPTER 3

FINANCIAL PREPARATION

Having pastored and mentored youths and teenagers for upward of 20 years, I can say without any fear of contradiction that one of the most talked about topics amongst young people is respect and financial freedom. Every young person is fantasising about that day when they will make so much 'bucks' that they will not be controlled by anyone else. No 'papa and mama' to tell them what to do and when to do it. They believe that respect will be accorded them when they have enough money to buy their own stuffs without resorting to having to ask anyone for money.

In a way, they are right. Someone once said, 'No man is truly independent until he is financially independent.' Pastor Matthew Ashimolowo said, as a parent of two young boys, 'As long as you eat my food, live in my house, sleep on the bed I bought, you have to do what I tell you to do.' The wisest man who has ever lived said, *"Money is a defence; it answers all things."*[45] So the quest and aspiration to make your own money is good and is actually encouraged.

Every young person should be taught the Art and Act of making money. Before we set into that however, let us clear some myths/misconceptions associated with money and being a Christian or child of God from the onset, so that we have an understanding of God's position from His manual as

> *Every young person should be taught the Art and Act of making money.*

---

[45] Ecclesiastes 7:12

it relates to our financial state.

1. God's will for us is that we prosper in spirit soul and body and materially. 3John 2 says *"Beloved, I wish above all things that thou mayest prosper and be in health, even as thy soul prospereth."* (KJV). It is a lie of the devil that being 'godly' is synonymous with poverty and Christians are supposed to be poor if they want to make heaven. Deuteronomy 8:18 says *"And you shall remember the Lord your God, for it is He who gives you power to get wealth, that He may establish His covenant which He swore to your fathers, as it is this day."* (NKJV).

2. The other myth is that paid employment secures my future, so I just need to go to school, get a degree and get a secured and well-paying job. This presupposes that once I get a job I will have enough money to take care of my needs. You might need to consider these statistics.
    - Over 90% of those in retirement in the UK cannot issue a cheque for any payment post retirement (Pastor Ashimolowo). They are in deep financial struggles.[46]
    - Paid employment reaffirms the notion that you must work for money rather than the prosperity paradigm of money working for you.
    - Recent economic meltdown and gross retrenchment of workers/staff in many companies world over.

3. Another misconception is that all rich people are crooks. The devil makes us believe that everyone of substance is either dodgy or shady in their dealings. As much as I will accept that, many rich young people get involved in shady deals/businesses, but we do have a good number of God fearing and God honouring young people who are wealthy.

4. Another myth is that a Christian must only focus on heaven and spiritual things. Well I believe that the next generation of kingdom expanders will be people who are not only heavenly conscious, but are also earthly useful and relevant.

5. Many young people believe in 'good luck' to make financial

---

[46]The Coming Wealth Transfer by Pastor Matthew Ashimolowo

breakthrough. They believe that one day luck will shine on them and they will suddenly come into some huge, life changing money and wealth. Research has shown that being wealthy is not a direct function of some luck. It is more of a carefully planned set of actions taken consistently over a period of time. Many people who have won big money either in the lottery or in some other means have, in a period of 3-5 years become worse off than they were before the windfall.[47]

The above listed myths and many more have over the years limited the scope of understanding of God's intention for us in regards to financial preparation and wealth generation. My sincere prayer and belief is for God to open our eyes of understanding and give us the willingness to appropriate His inexhaustible provisions in our lives. Myles Munroe once said, 'When the purpose of a thing is not understood, abuse is inevitable.' Many young people are not very happy with their parents' financial state now and unless we do something about it, the next generation will demand more from us.

A. LEARN HOW TO MAKE MONEY EARLY

The earlier you learn how to make money, the better for your tomorrow. Acquire the knowledge that is required to make money early. Ask questions from people who have a proven track record of financial success. Surround yourself with people who can help challenge your perspective on finance and stretch you to achieve your full potentials. Read books about making money and about great entrepreneurs who started from scratch and have grown great financial estates. Most importantly renew your mind from fallacies being peddled as wisdom. Come into the position where you appreciate the fact that your state in life is often a matter of personal choice.

B. GET KNOWLEDGE

To be financially independent in your tomorrow, you need to acquire the information and skills of how money works and how to make it. Reading through the book Rich Dad and Poor Dad by Robert Kiyosaki, it is obvious that the conventional schools we all

---

[47] The Curse Of The Lotto. How The Millions Can Ruin Lives by Complex.

attend tend to prepare us to be 'enslaved' to work for money. Rich people teach their children/wards at home and through their enterprises on how to create jobs and get money to work for them, thereby making money their servants and slaves[48]. He went on to say that, 'If you want to thrive in today's economy, you must challenge the status quo and get the financial education necessary to succeed.'[49]

C. DESIRE TO BE WEALTHY

This is a no-brainer really. You must have a desire to be rich and wealthy. In the book, The Richest Man in Babylon, it is stated that the riches of Babylon were the results of the wisdom of its people. They first had to learn how to become wealthy.

D. ACTIVELY LOOK OUT FOR OPPORTUNITIES, SEIZE THEM AND USE THEM

Arkad, the richest man in Babylon, when asked how he moved from abject poverty to become so rich, said, 'By taking advantage of opportunities available to all citizens of our good city.' It never ceases to amaze me how many people, living in great and highly advanced cities of the world, with limitless opportunities but remain poor. The United States of America is called 'the land of opportunities, where dreams really do come true.' The United Kingdom is full of different opportunities to make money in the most legitimate way and young people are failing to avail themselves of such. I pray and believe God to help the next generation to begin to take advantage of numerous opportunities available to create a secured financial tomorrow for you.

SAVINGS AND INVESTMENT

There are broadly speaking two schools of thoughts when it comes to savings and investments as Christians. There are those who believe that whatever they make today should be spent solving today's issues and problems, believing that tomorrow will take care

---

[48] Rich Dad,Poor Dad. Robert Kiyosaki
[49] Rich Dad, Poor Dad. Robert Kiyosaki

of itself. They quote bible passages such as Matthew 6:25 that says, *"Therefore I say to you, do not worry about your life, what you will eat or what you will drink; nor about your body, what you will put on. Is not life more than food and the body more than clothing,"* to buttress their point.

The second school of thought belongs to those who say we need to save for the proverbial 'rainy day'. Make savings and wise investments even for our children and generations to come. They also quote bible passages such as Proverbs 13:22 which says, *"A good man leaves an inheritance for his children's children, but the wealth of the sinner is stored up for the righteous,"* to support their stance. Whichever side of the divide you belong to, I want to just give you three right reasons to invest and three wrong reasons to invest as a Christian.

RIGHT REASONS FOR INVESTING

1. Multiply To Give More: Looking at the parable of the talents as told by Jesus in Luke 19:12-26. *"Therefore He said: "A certain nobleman went into a far country to receive for himself a kingdom and to return. 13 So he called ten of his servants, delivered to them ten minas,[a] and said to them, 'Do business till I come.' 14 But his citizens hated him, and sent a delegation after him, saying, 'We will not have this man to reign over us."*

15 And so it was that when he returned, having received the kingdom, he then commanded these servants, to whom he had given the money, to be called to him, that he might know how much every man had gained by trading. 16 Then came the first, saying, 'Master, your mina has earned ten minas.' 17 And he said to him, 'Well done, good servant; because you were faithful in a very little, have authority over ten cities.' 18 And the second came, saying, 'Master, your mina has earned five minas.' 19 Likewise he said to him, 'You also be over five cities.'

20 Then another came, saying, 'Master, here is your mina, which I have kept put away in a handkerchief. 21 For I feared you, because you are an austere man. You collect what you did not deposit, and reap what you did not sow.' 22 And he said to him, 'Out of your own mouth I will judge you, you wicked servant. You knew that I was an austere man, collecting what I did not deposit and reaping what I did not sow. 23 Why then did you not put my money in the bank, that at my coming I might have collected it with interest?'

24 And he said to those who stood by, 'Take the mina from him, and give it to him who has ten minas.' 25 (But they said to him, 'Master, he has ten minas.') 26 'For I say to you, that to everyone who has will be given; and from him who does not have, even what he has will be taken away from him."

This parable from Jesus tells us that God entrusts wealth to some of his stewards so that it will be available to Him at a later date. The management of wealth requires that it be invested or multiplied, as the parable reflects.

2. To Meet Future Family Needs: God in His word enjoins us to provide for our family in future. Every young man would eventually become a husband and father tomorrow. To be able to fulfil this assignment, the youth of today requires the sacrifice of some short-range spending to meet future needs, such as education, housing or start in business. Furthermore good planning requires laying aside some of the surplus of today for future needs. Proverbs 6:6-8 says, *"Go to the ant, you sluggard, consider her ways and be wise, which having no captain, overseer or ruler, provides her supplies in the summer and gathers her food in the harvest.".*

It is important to realise that the attainment of good education for the future generation cannot be over emphasised. I remember telling my youth church members 15 years ago that while they are asking their parents to buy them higher education notebooks for writing, their children will be asking for electronic tablets, iPads and other gadgets and they better should be prepared financially.

3. **To Further The Gospel And Fund Special Needs:** The next generation of kingdom takers and expanders must learn to give to causes that will promote the gospel. Additional needs come up that require special funding. These include building programs, special emergency relief funds, and opportunities to help the needy amongst us. How many times have a Christian like you wanted to help someone in need and you are incapacitated yourself? If the church is ever to break out of the poverty mentality, then Christians must have enough to invest and be willing to give to legitimate needs. May God make you and I, the channel of blessing to someone today. May we be the answer to someone else's prayers in Jesus' name.

WRONG REASONS TO INVEST

Have you really observed that giving is not as easy as you can make more money; it is actually more difficult. Stingy people don't get more benevolent as they prosper, they get increasingly stingy. With that in mind, let us look at 3 wrong reasons for investing

1. Greed: Greed means we always want more than we need. We must decide and acknowledge right from the onset of our youthful life that God is our source. If we lose sight of that truth, no amount will be enough. At some point we must stop and ask ourselves how much is actually enough for us, and also ask ourselves why we are trying to make and store more money. The unbelievers of our days (and years to come) are not impressed by how much a Christian can make and keep. The one thing that does impress them is someone who gives away everything for what he/she believes in. It has been said that 'People don't care how much you know, until they know how much you care.'[50]

It has been proven statistically that the number one reason why most people lose money in investment is because of greed. The get-rich quick con- men typically relies and plays on our greed to blindfold and subsequently dupe us. For anyone whoever wants to get something for nothing, will always end up getting nothing for something. So be clear about your motive and be brutally honest with yourself and God about it. Never let greed be your reason for wanting money.

2. Slothfulness/laziness: It is quite surprising that slothfulness might be a motive to investing, but it is. The desire to make in one day what you should have planned to make over a period of time. Many Christians are not diligent enough to plan well for their tomorrow, and when, inevitably the tomorrow comes, they start panicking and begin to make hasty decisions including financial ones. I have met some fine Christians in my time that play the lottery religiously with the hope that they will hit a jackpot someday. Well I am still waiting for such breakthrough.

A regular habit of spending less than you make (no matter what you make) and saving the difference is the best investment plan. Hasty speculations, on the other hand, are characterized in Proverbs 20:4 which says, *"The lazy man will not plow because of winter; he will beg during harvest and have nothing."* Please plan well for tomorrow. 'What about tomorrow?' should always be the question

---

[50] Theodore Roosevelt, Politician and 26th American President

asked. The story of Joseph Jacob in Genesis 41:33-36 is very apt.

33 "Therefore, Pharaoh should find an intelligent and wise man and put him in charge of the entire land of Egypt. 34 Then Pharaoh should appoint supervisors over the land and let them collect one-fifth of all the crops during the seven good years. 35 Have them gather all the food produced in the good years that are just ahead and bring it to Pharaoh's storehouses. Store it away, and guard it so there will be food in the cities. 36 That way there will be enough to eat when the seven years of famine come to the land of Egypt. Otherwise this famine will destroy the land." (NLT).

3. Ego/pride:[51] Many people, including Christians, invest to bolster their pride and ego. They just want to be proud, to be the money man/woman around. They love to let everyone see how wealthy they are. Proverbs 29:23 says, *"A man's pride will bring him low, but the humble in spirit will retain honour."* Let us be humble despite what God has put in our care. We should realise that all that we have has been given to us by God and for his purpose.

I wish I could give to you, dear reader, one line of advice that will solve any financial problem and secure a robust tomorrow for you. But if the truth must be told, there is no magical 'almighty' formula to wealth, rather what we have is a combination of factors and principles that can and will progressively move you in the direction of financial independence. Let us therefore painstakingly look at these principles with a view to practising them for ultimate result.

INVEST IN YOURSELF

Investing in yourself means you make deliberate decisions to better and position yourself to be financially secured tomorrow. It starts with acquiring knowledge about the world of finance. It involves being financially intelligent. It entails arming yourself with the required wisdom to create and maintain wealth. This often involves acquiring sound education. You might need more than one type of education as explained in chapter 2. Jacob in Genesis 30:30b asked the question of his uncle and employer then, *"And now when shall I provide for mine own house also?"* Jacob was not only in the employment of Laban, but he was also having a non-formal

---

[51] Investing For The Future by Larry Burkett

type of education. He was learning the very lucrative trade of cattle production and rearing. He had to learn all that needed to be learnt for him to become wealthy on his own. He invested years into that 'schooling' or apprenticeship.

Whatever you are learning now is an investment in your tomorrow. Whether you are in a formal education studying or learning a trade. Jim Rohn said, 'Formal education will make you a living; self - education will make you a fortune.'[52] It is actually the greatest investment you can make. Do it faithfully and diligently. Learn all that needs to be learnt. Know everything and much more that needs to be known. There is no shortcut to success. Every shortcut has a way of cutting you short. Also importantly, is the diligence and faithfulness with which you handle someone else's business and investment. The world, more than at any other time, is looking for faithful people. Be a person of proven integrity. Let your employer trust you.

The book of Proverbs 20:6 says, *"Most men will proclaim each his own goodness, but who can find a faithful man?"* Unfortunately, gone are the days when people trust anyone who goes to church to do business with. There is so much lack of trust even amongst fellow church members. But I believe that you and I can bring such trust back by being faithful in our own little corners. Let our yes be yes and our no be no. Let our bosses and trainers be confident that their businesses are safe with us. Paul, in admonishing a young man in his days said, *"Let no one despise your youth, but be an example to the believers, in word, in conduct, in love, in spirit, in faith, and in purity."* 1 Timothy 4:12. Invest in your integrity. Be honest with whatever has been committed into your hands. Luke 6:11 says, *"If you have not been faithful in the unrighteous mammon, who will commit to your trust true riches?"*

Read books like 'Rich Dad Poor Dad', by Robert Kiyosaki Think and Grow Rich, by Napoleon Hill and The Richest Man in Babylon, etc., that gives you great insight into the world of financial literacy. Buy books that typify your destiny. Read the book of Proverbs and Ecclesiastes by Solomon David Jesse, the wisest man to have ever lived. I am always surprised when people complain about lack of finance, yet they do not have one book on finance to learn from. Proverbs 23;23 says, *"Buy the truth and do not sell, also*

---

[52] Jim Rohn

wisdom and instructions and understanding."

Two things more than anything else determine your destiny in life; the books you read and the company you keep. Proverbs 13;20 says, *"He who walks with wise men will be wise but the companion of fools will be destroyed."* 1 Corinthians 15:33 says, *"Be not deceived, evil company corrupts good habits."* So investing in yourself includes being honest, building your character, moving with the wise, and reading books that will help you.

BORROW SPARINGLY

One of the ways to prepare and secure a financial future is to learn from your youth how to borrow sparingly or not at all. This is a big mistake that has been passed down young people by the older generation especially in the developed economies of the world. We have been taught to always buy now and pay later. Adverts flood our television screens encouraging us to buy things that we do not need because we are not paying now. Please learn how to avoid debt like a plague.

There are people who spend more than 20% of their income servicing the debt they have. They cannot afford to be without a job or their business for a month. In the words of the poor; 'I owe, I owe and so to work I go'[53].

Once you start out yourself on an ocean of red ink, buying things you cannot afford to pay for, and having lines of credit for everything, it means you are living beyond your means and are spending the money you have not earned. Proverbs 22:7 says, *"The rich ruleth over the poor, and the borrower is a slave to the lender."*(KJV). The rule of the thumb is to buy only what you can afford. Never spend the money you don't have. Will Smith, famous Hollywood Actor was once quoted as saying, 'Too many people spend the money they haven't earned, to buy things they don't need, to impress

> **The rule of the thumb is to buy only what you can afford. Never spend the money you don't have.**

---

[53] The Coming Wealth Transfer by Pastor Matthew Ashimolowo

people they don't like.'[54]

PAY YOURSELF FIRST

Always try to pay yourself from whatever income you generate. Do not spend all that comes into your hand. This is especially true for those in business. The temptation to believe or assume that all the money you get is yours is always there. Have a system in place to differentiate between the company's money and your disposable income, that is money that you can spend on yourself. Pay yourself a regular income and be disciplined enough to avoid tampering with the company's finances. People have been sent to jail for crimes in that regard. Another advantage of paying yourself is that it helps you determine what you are actually worth and if need be, work on increasing and improving your worth and value.

PROTECT YOURSELF AND YOUR LOVED ONES

Get Insurances. I am a firm believer in the grace of God to keep and protect us, I also believe in using all the available resources at my disposal to protect not just myself but my loved ones. By the grace of God, my first degree is in Insurance and Actuarial Science, so I am very aware of the importance of having the right insurances in place for myself and my family and I have from a very early age put Insurance policies in place to take care of my most loved ones, not just in death but in case of accidental injury and loss of earning as a self- employed person. The rule of thumb is talk to professionals who will help you decide what type of cover you need and do it early.

GIVE GENEROUSLY

The importance of learning how to give from our youth cannot be over emphasised. It is not debatable that it is very important to be a giver and learn how to work in what I call the 'giver's grace'. There are loads of blessings that you receive by being a giver. Be

---

[54] Will Smith, American Hollywood Actor

liberal in giving. Proverbs 11:24-25 says, *"There is one who scatters, yet increases more; and there is one who withholds more than is right, but it leads to poverty. The generous soul will be made rich and he who waters will also be watered himself."* The principle of the world is for us to gather as much as we possibly can to ourselves, but the principle of God is to give generously as much as we possibly can. It there is any one truth that cannot be exaggerated, it is the principle of giving. It works in any situation and at all times, irrespective of whether you are a 'Christian' or not. Giving is like sowing, and as early as in Genesis 8:22, God said, *"While the earth remains, seedtime and harvest, cold and heat, winter and summer, and day and not shall not cease."*

If you sow, you will reap. I know a lot of doctrines are out there in regard to giving to God, ministers, etc, and many of the so called ministers are mainly out to milk and exploit the gullibility of their members, but the principle of God stands sure. I will encourage Christians to search the scripture and discover what is the true plan and purpose of God about giving.

For the purpose of this book, I have identified three groups of people that your giving should be directed to for optimum result of God's continual blessing.

A) Giving to God. Giving to God has taken a variety of meaning depending on who is saying it. But as a young person preparing for financial independence and abundance, it cannot be ignored. Giving to God comes in two major ways. Tithe and offering, and giving to missions.

Ai) Tithe. Tithe has been variously described to mean 10% of your disposable earning. Others say it is 10% of your gross earning, yet others say it is 10% of whatever you earn. Tithe paying has come under serious attack in recent times, mainly because of the sometimes erroneous interpretations and imbalanced teaching given to it by some pastors. I have heard some pastors say that 'you will go to hell if you do not pay tithe.' Some church members have been scared to a point of wizardry in regards to their 'obligation' and responsibility to pay tithe. Some Christians also argue that tithe paying is an Old Testament arrangement which has no bearing whatsoever in the New Testament.

I personally, with the help of the Holy Spirit have discovered that the issue of paying tithe from the scriptural perspective is very easy. Tithe means 10% of your earning being voluntarily given to

God, through the agency of the Church, for the use of the church. It is an expression of our love for God, who has willingly and freely given us all things.

For a better understanding of the issue of tithe, let us consider what theologians call the Law of First Mention. Tithe was first mentioned in Genesis 14:18-20. *"Then Melchizedek king of Salem brought out bread and wine; he was the priest of God Most High. And he blessed him and said: 'Blessed be Abram of God Most High, Possessor of heaven and earth; and blessed be God Most High, who has delivered your enemies into your hand.' And he gave him a tithe of al.,"* Furthermore in Genesis 28:20-22, *"Then Jacob made a vow, saying, 'If God will be with me, and keep me in this way that I am going, and give me bread to eat and clothing to put on, so that I come back to my father's house in peace, then the Lord shall be my God. And this stone which I have set as a pillar shall be God' house, and of all that You give me I will surely give a tenth to You.'"*

So we can deduce from the above that tithe is a voluntary arrangement between two parties. It is very important to have the right attitude towards tithing. Avoid these three unhealthy attitudes;

(a). Tithing out of obligation. Remember, Abraham tithed out of free will, long before God commanded it.

(b). Limiting God. Remember that all that you have is God's, not just the 10%. 'When I give 10%, God blesses the remaining 90% and multiplies it.' Bishop David Oyedepo said, 'Tithe is God's portion which makes the remainder meaningful.'

> *Tithe is God's portion which makes the remainder meaningful.*

(c). Conditional tithing. Don't predicate your tithing on the condition that God is obliged to meet your needs. You do not tithe to meet a need, you tithe to obey. Start practising tithing from your young age. Do it as a spiritual discipline; do it consistently and systematically. On a final note, if you have neglected to pay tithe in the past, forget what you 'owe' God (you can never repay God anyway!).

Obey God starting from today. Also know that the blessings mentioned in the bible are not just financial. After all, there is more to life than money. Each time you tithe, carefully observe how God blesses you, even in things that money cannot buy. Malachi 3:10-12 says, *"Bring all tithes into the storehouse, that there may be food in my house, and try Me now in this' says the Lord of hosts, 'If I will not open for you the windows of heaven and pour out for you such blessing that there will not be room enough to receive it. And I will rebuke the devourer for your sakes, so that he will not destroy the fruit of your ground, nor the vine shall fail to bear fruit for you in the field ' says the Lord of hosts; 'And all nations will call you blessed, for you will be a delightful land' says the Lord of hosts."*

In summary, the issue of tithing can be summarised in the following statement:

Abraham commenced it (Genesis 14:17-20)
Jacob continued it (Genesis 28:22)
Moses commanded it (Leviticus 27:30-32)
Malachi confirmed it (Malachi 3:8-12)
Jesus commended it (Matthew 23:23)
So who am I to condemn it?[55]

Aii) Offering. Offering is what you give over and above your tithe. Never, if you really and sincerely can, appear before God empty handed. Always be ready to give to God and his cause on a consistent basis. How you should give your offerings;

(a). Give decidedly and willingly, never out of compulsion. 2 Corinthians, 9:6-7 says *'But this I say: He who sows sparingly will also reap sparingly and he who sows bountifully will also reap bountifully. So let each one give as he purposes in his heart, not grudgingly or of necessity; for God loves a cheerful giver."*

(b). Give Liberally. This tests your heart. 2 Corinthians 8:1-4 says, *"Moreover, brethren, we make known to you the grace of God bestowed on the churches of Macedonia; that in a great trial of affliction the abundance of their joy and their deep poverty abounded in the riches of their liberality. For I bear witness that according to their ability, and yes beyond their ability they were freely willing, imploring us with much urgency that we would receive the gift and the fellowship of the ministering to the saints."*

(c). Give Bountifully. This talks about the amount. Luke 6:38 says, *"Give, and it will be given to you: good measure pressed down, shaken together, and running over will be put into your bosom. For with the same measure that you use, it will be measured back to you."*

55

iv. Give consistently. This talks about the frequency of your giving. Ecclesiastes 11:6 says, *"In the morning sow your seed and in the evening do not withhold your hand; for you do not know which will prosper, either this or that or whether both alike will be good."*

GIVING TO MINISTERS AND MISSION WORK

This is very important, as the gospel needs to be taken to the ends of the earth, and that requires a lot of finance. The Lord trusts you and I, having being blessed, to make finances available for the gospel. Philippians 4:15-19 says, *"Now you Philippians know that in the beginning of the gospel, when I departed from Macedonia, no church shared with me concerning giving and receiving but you only. For even in Thessalonica you sent aid once and again for my necessities. Not that I seek the gift, but I seek the fruit that abounds to your account. Indeed I have all and abound. I am full, having received from Epaphroditus the things sent from you, a sweet-smelling aroma, an acceptable sacrifice, well pleasing to God. And my God shall supply all your needs according to His riches in glory by Christ Jesus."*

GIVING TO YOUR PARENTS

The second aspect of giving generously is giving to your parents. You are commanded to take care of your parents by God. 'If your parents took care of you until you started growing your teeth, you must take care of them when they start to lose theirs.'[56] It is a covenant thing with God when you take it upon yourself to constantly and fastidiously give to your parents. You honour them by so doing and consequently attract God's blessing on your live. The first commandment with a promise is that of honouring our parents. Exodus 20:12 says, *"Honour your father and mother. Then you will live a long, full life in the land the Lord your God is giving you."* (NLT). The promise of God in this passage is two–pronged; Quantity of life, (you will live long) and Quality of Life, (you will live a full live). If you literally take God at His word here, and be a blessing to your parents, you are securing for yourself a glorious future.

---

[56] Chinese proverb

CONCLUSION

The importance for financial preparation for our tomorrow as youth cannot be over emphasised. The issue of money and finance play an important role in the stability and wellbeing of our house. Like Mr. Jacob Isaac asked in Genesis,[30] *"When will I prepare for my own house also?"* We need to start asking that question very early and then take practical steps to securing our financial future. I believe that with God on your side and the application of your God-given wisdom, we will not just be blessed but we shall become a source of blessing to others around us.

I pray and declare by the spirit of the Lord that the spirit of knowledge, wisdom, understanding, and the fear of God will take over your life and teach you to create wealth, that will be perpetuated into generation. The bible says, a good man leaves an inheritance for his children's children; I pray and proclaim that you will not die in poverty. You will not only be wealthy in your lifetime, but your generation will be wealthy in riches and even in things that money cannot buy. You will build and leave houses for your children, you will leave wealth in the order of Abraham for your children and they shall call you blessed.

See you at the top!

CHAPTER 4

MARITAL PREPARATION

'Happy is the man who finds a true friend, and far happier is he who finds that true friend in his wife.'

- Franz Schubert

One of the most important decisions you will ever make is the choice of who to marry and spend the rest of your life with. The plan of God in setting up the institution of marriage is for a MAN and a WOMAN to live together in a union basically for the purpose of companionship and procreation amongst other things.

Please note that marriage as instituted by God is between a male and a female, that is between John and Janet, not between Bob and Billy or Lizzie and Jessica. God himself said, in Genesis 2:18, *"It is not good for the man to be alone..."* And he proceeded to make him a help-meet. Billy Graham said, "The Bible is very clear, God's definition of marriage is between a man and a woman.'[57] So it is safe to conclude that it was God's original intention and plan to institute marriage.

How then do you prepare for this very important stage of life? What steps need to be taken to ensure that this very essential, often life-altering decision is taken very seriously? If you have been around for a little while, you would have noticed without fail, the sustained attack on the marriage institution. There is the arsenal of hell being unleashed, on a continuous basis, on marriages over the ages. A little peek into recent statistics will either shock you or confirm your worst fears about marriage.

---

[57] Billy Graham.- American Evangelist

DIVORCE RATES AND REASONS

Divorce statistics in the last 10 years around the world make a gruesome reading. Statistics in the last 10 years around the world put the United States of America and the United Kingdom at the top of the table of the highest divorce rates of the world. The United Kingdom has the highest divorce rate in the European Union, which are 2.8 divorces per 1000 marriages.[58] Rates of childbirth outside wedlock and marriage are 38% in the United Kingdom compared to 4% in Greece.

Generally speaking, divorce rate is 200 times higher than just a century ago. According to TopFor research, divorce means the life partners get separated from each other for a lifetime. It is true to say that divorce is a slap on the face of our societies; it accompanies destruction of not only two lives, but also two families. The reasons for divorce can be varying, such as the lack of mental compatibility, lesser mutual interactions, no babies, financial issues, lack of commitment, lack of communication between partners, infidelity, abandonment, substance or alcohol abuse, sexual and emotional abuse, inability to manage and resolve conflicts and lack of maturity, etc. [59]

Research has also shown that divorce often happens because people rarely discuss their expectations in detail prior to marriage and less willing to work on their marriage afterwards. They like quick fix solutions rather than having to resolve issues. People have gotten divorced for trivial issues like what side of the bed to sleep on and what part of the toothpaste tube to start pressing from. Funny, isn't it? It went on to list the top 10 countries with the highest divorce rates in 2014 as follows:

1. United States of America
2. United Kingdom
3. Aruba
4. South Africa
5. Italy
6. Ukraine
7. Russia
8. South Korea

---

[58] Daily Mail Online
[59] Topfor Magazine. June 2014

9. India
10. Canada[60]

Reading through that list quickly points two things out to me. One is that most of these countries are predominantly Christian populated or dominated countries. Secondly, they are either developed or developing economies of the world. This means that spiritually, the devil is strategic about the countries he is attacking. He is on a mission to target Christian Homes which should form the nucleus of a well-balanced society.

The devil is breaking homes with reckless abandon, and children and youth who should have been brought up in the nurture and admonition of the Lord are being left to their whims and caprices. But the devil is a liar. We are going to raise strong families in our generation where the fear of the Lord, which is the beginning of wisdom, will be taught and instituted. Amen.

So what do we need to do to prepare for this great union and avoid the pitfalls of the past, since God has expressly said in His manual that he hates divorce? Malachi 2:16 says, *"For the LORD God of Israel says that He hates divorce…"*

STEPS TO A SUCCESSFUL MARRIAGE

1. UNDERSTAND WHAT MARRIAGE IS

This might sound and look obvious, but you will be surprised about the number of young people who get married with little or no information about what they are getting into. This reminds me of the saying of Jesus in Luke 14:28, which says, *"For which of you intending to build a tower does not first sit down and count the cost whether he has enough to finish it?"*

Get enough knowledge about what a good marriage is. Find out what constitutes success in marriage. For the purpose of this book and the sake of simplicity and clarity, I will liken a good marriage to a good fruit, which is a product of a healthy tree which in turn is the end product of a healthy seed. Jesus said in Matthew 12:33, *"Make a tree good and its fruit will be good. And make a tree bad and its fruit will be bad, for a tree is recognised by its fruit."* This means for most

---

[60] topFor Magazine April, 2014

53

> *A good marriage is like a good fruit, which is a product of a healthy tree which in turn is the end*

marriages that end in divorce, the seed has been sown many years before the marriage was ever consummated, albeit unknowingly. Every marriage is a product of many influences and forces over a long period of time.

Seven major forces that influence marriages have been statistically highlighted as:

i. Values
ii. Roles and responsibilities
iii. Habits and Irritations
iv. Past Hurts
v. People
vi. Parasites
vii. Personal attitudes

i. Values

This means the regard in which something is held. It talks about your ideas about marriage. It connotes the importance, worth or usefulness of something. It is the principles or standard code of behaviour. Values are important and lasting beliefs or ideas shared by the members of a culture about what is good or bad, desirable or undesirable about a thing. It has been proven through research that, children who grow up in households where their parents are married view marriages more positively than those who grew up with divorced, separated or non-married cohabitating parents.

Children of divorced or cohabitating parents are more likely to cohabitate with their respective partners in the future rather than commit to marriage.[61]

So our view of marriage is directly shaped by how our parents lived in their own marriage. Children of violent and abusive fathers in a marriage have been known to grow and believe that is the norm. A note of caution to parents here. The way you are living now is a testimony and a pattern for your children to follow. Make sure it is a good example you are laying. Let us give our children the good legacy of values in marriage.

---

[61] Cunningham & Thornton (2005)

54

ii. Roles and responsibilities

This is another factor that influences marriages. What are the traditional and conventional roles and responsibilities of the parties in marriage. We live in an age where everyone is an individual and can do whatever they like. God specifically created man and gave him a job to do before He gave him a wife to marry. He instructed him to cultivate the ground. Man was told to protect and to always be in His presence and worship Him. The woman on the other hand is to be a help-meet; to complement and complete the man; to advise and support him. Any negation of the roles either by the individuals or the society at large will result in chaos.

Similar expectations of work roles, house roles and spouse roles are some of the most important factors in a marriage. If both spouses are traditional, that works wonderfully as it does if both are contemporary. The greatest conflicts occur when wives are more contemporary than their husbands in what they consider the 'right' roles for husbands and wives and vice versa.

iii. Habits and irritations

We are all creatures of habits. The things we do repeatedly over a period of time become our habits. When you bring two people from different backgrounds in a long lasting union like marriage, we must expect that there will be a lot of clashes. Many of us, over the years have gathered some annoying habits that can be very irritating. The ability and maturity to accommodate the other person's habits are very crucial in marriages . Many of these habits can be cultural, religious and so on. For instance, I know some cultures where it is a sign of great disrespect for a child to either be looking straight at an older person's eyes when being spoken to, whereas it is a sure sign of lying or not being interested in the discussion in another culture.

iv. Past hurts

These affect marriages when we bring in our past hurts and experiences into the present. If a person has suffered say, physical, sexual and emotional abuse as a child, it is a little harder to trust people later on in life as an adult. Research indicates that an individual who had a happy or normal childhood is more likely to succeed in marriage than children who had a rough time growing up. Never let your past experiences be a hindrance to fulfilling a

> *Never let your past experiences be a hindrance to fulfilling a good life in the present and in the future.*

good life in the present and in the future. Leave your past in the past. You cannot do anything about it. Just let it go. Face the present and the future with renewed hope.

v. People

We are all social creatures. We are designed by the creator to do better when we relate more with people. Over an individual's life, you come across so many people who influence your perspective. From our parents when growing up, to our teachers in schools, our religious leaders, colleagues and friends; we are being influenced, sometimes, unknowingly. We might not be able to do anything about the choice of some people like parents and siblings, teachers etc, but we can do a great deal with our choice of other people like friends and colleagues. We should be very concerned with the type of people we allow into our cycle and sphere of influence. Who we allow to speak into our lives, teach and mentor us is a matter of choice. Learn how to identify and walk with the right people that will motivate and inspire you.

For instance, as a young man aspiring or intending to marry, you should deliberately surround yourself with people who are married and making great stride at making their marriage a continuous success.

vi. Parasites

Parasites are defined as organisms which lives in or on other organisms (its host) and benefits by deriving nutrients at the others' expense. These are things or people that are not beneficial in any way, shape or form to your future marriage and they are also milking you dry. They only survive by extracting nutrients and support from you. These include wide range of bad habits like gambling, masturbation, alcohol and drug abuse, pornography and other negative vices that can and will jeopardise your future marriage.

The advice is to seek both spiritual and medical help before getting married as it will get worse NOT better after marriage.

Other forms of parasites are people who are selfish and out only for their personal interest. The only motivation they have is 'What is in it for me.' Detach yourself from such by all means necessary.

vii. Personal attitudes

Obviously, the personality of the individuals involved in a marriage is one of the most crucial factors affecting it. Traits such as emotional stability, self- control, affection, responsibility, favourable self-perception and optimism are correlated with good marriage adjustments. For instance, a democratic attitude, where both parties seek to cooperate and compromise is most functional compared to the autocratic and dictatorial attitude of most men in marriage where they are the Lord and master that can and should never be questioned. It is most important to develop a positive attitude to things in life. Have a working and practical faith in the goodness and grace of God.

Some people in life always see the good in every situation. Their slogan is, 'It could be worse,' while others always see the evil in all and every situation. Some look for and see opportunities in every adversity, while others see adversity in in every opportunity. Romans 8:28 says, *"And we know that all things work together for good to them that love God and are called according to His purpose."* It did not say that everything that happens to you will be good, but that in everything that happens, whether classified as good or bad, believe that it will ultimately turn around for your good.

Understand that marriage is not for boys and girls, but for young men and women who are not only matured physically, but emotionally, psychologically, spiritually and financially. Research has shown that people who get married between the ages of 23-27 are more likely to stay together than teenagers. In my few years of dealing with young people, I'm always intrigued to discover boys and girls who can hardly take care of themselves, talking and rushing into marriage. I have counselled a number of youths who do not have a clue about how and what to do in real life marriage situations, but are hell-bent on marrying because God has 'spoken' to them.

Also fundamental to any successful marriage is the kind of man or woman you marry. Let us settle this once and for all from inception, never marry someone who is not spiritually compatible with you. Someone who does not have the same faith as you, as a

Christian, is forbidden. If you are a Christian, please marry a Christian. Someone put it succinctly, 'If you marry the devil's son or daughter, you cannot prevent the father-in-law from visiting.'

> *If you marry the devil's son or daughter, you cannot prevent the father-in-law from visiting.*

Marry someone who has the same vision of where you are going. Abraham, who is regarded as the father of faith, had to instruct his servant not to marry a wife from among the unbelievers for his son Isaac. Genesis 24:1-4 says, *"Now Abraham was old, well advanced in age; and the Lord had blessed Abraham in all things. So Abraham said to the oldest servant of his house, who ruled over all that he had, 'please, put your hand under my thigh, and I will make you swear by the LORD, the God of heaven, and the God of the earth, that you will not take a wife for my son from the daughters of the Canaanites among whom I dwell; but you shall go to my country and my family and take a wife for my son Isaac.'"* Here we can see how important it is to marry someone who has the same vision as you and understands you enough to stay with you and help you build a good future. If Abraham, who is regarded as the father of faith, had enough sense to do this, then I think it is worth emulating.

2. BE INTENTIONAL ABOUT GETTING MARRIED

You cannot be passive about life. You must be intentional about your future home. Someone once said, 'The best way to predict the future is to make it happen.'[62] Many get married without being intentional about it. No plan whatsoever. They just settled for the quickest, cheapest, easiest and most readily available option. So what does it mean to be intentional? To be intentional means to be focused, not easily distracted and confident. Intentional people are careful planners. They are sound. They are on a journey to a better, greater future. Let us look at 4 statements of an intentional youth preparing for marital bliss:

A. I am interested but not desperate

---

[62] Mike Murdoch

B. I am available but not cheap
C. I am the chooser, not just the chosen
D. I look and listen before I leap.[63]

A. I am interested but not desperate

In Matthew 13:44-46, Jesus, in the parable of the hidden treasure, said, *"Again, the kingdom of heaven is like treasure hidden in a field, which a man found and hid; and for joy over it he goes and sells all that he has and buys that field. Again the kingdom of heaven is like a merchant seeking beautiful pearls who, when he had found one pearl of great price, went and sold all that he had and bought it."*

To be interested is to be attracted to or pay attention to someone or something. To be desperate on the other hand is to have critical need for someone of something. It is to demonstrate hopelessness or to act recklessly. To be interested in marriage is to be doing something about marriage from now. Start praying long and hard before you are ready to marry. Not just when you are of age. Attend seminars; study the lives of enviable and exemplary marriages around. Be mentored by people in successful relationships. Read books about marriages. There must be corresponding action to back up your faith that you will get married. James 2:17 says, *"This also faith by itself, if it does not have works, is dead."*

Mike Murdock said, 'The proof of desire is pursuit.' Be on an honest quest for a godly life partner. Look in the right places and meet right people. Attend youth meetings. Go to camps and conventions, not just pubs and dancehalls. An African proverb says, 'If you pick a wife on the dance floor, she will eventually go with the crowd.' If you do all of the above mentioned, you will not become desperate, but will also identify 'desperadoes' when they show up.

B. I am available but not cheap

Proverbs 31:10 says, *"Who can find a virtuous wife? For her worth is far above rubies."* To be available means to be accessible and obtainable. You are not out of reach. But to be cheap means you are inexpensive, worth and cost relatively little, of poor quality and not worthy of respect. For every young person preparing to marry,

---

[63] Dr. Tayo Adeyemi.- Founding/ Senior Pastor, New Wine Church, London

don't ever put yourself in a position where anyone thinks they can have you at whatever price. Place a high value on yourself. When you place a high value on yourself, three things are quickly established.

i. Not everybody can have me: It is safe to say that everyone has a pair of shoes, but it is also safe to say not everyone has a Ferrari. It means you are not available to every Tom, Dick and Harry, or every Rhoda, Janet and Lizzie. You filter out the wrong people. You give yourself some respect. Let people know that you are a high quality product straight from the manufacturer's factory. You are an original, not a copy. You are a prince/princess of the most high God. You are not just some worthless article.

ii. No room for experimentation or sampling: When something is cheap, people will sample it even when they know they have no intention of buying it. The reason why people get sampled and dumped is because they didn't cost much. Jacob placed such a high value on Rachel that he was willing to work and wait seven years for her and when he was deceived and given Leah instead, he was willing to work and wait another seven years and it seemed like just a few days to him. Genesis 29:20 says, *"So Jacob served seven years to get Rachel, but it seemed like only a few days to him, because of his love for her."* Waiting is one proof of love. I usually say to young ladies that if any man cannot wait for the wedding night to have sex with you, he's not worthy of your love.

iii. No Room For Negotiation: I am a businessman with years of experience behind me. One rule of business is negotiation and the rule of thumb in negotiation is to never pay the full price. You always want to get a bargain. To achieve this, you have to resort to saying things like; 'I have seen it cheaper somewhere else,' just to devalue the product in before the seller. In preparing for marriage, do not let anyone devalue you just to 'have' you. When they say you are not that beautiful, and other girls are willing to have sex before marriage with them, remember to tell them that, *"you are fearfully and wonderfully made,"* and that, *"you are a chosen generation, a royal priesthood, a holy nation, a peculiar people…"* I Peter 2:9. Tell them to go to those girls.

I'm reminded of the story of a guy who asked a young lady if she would have sex with him for £1,000,000. The lady said yes. Then the guy said, 'What about for £50?' to which the lady replied, 'What kind of lady do you think I am?' The guy laughed and said,

'We have already established that, we are just trying to fix a figure.' Don't ever lower your price just to satisfy any devilish intent. Many young ladies wear their price tags on their heads. To beat a negotiator, tell him to go and buy the product where he has seen it cheaper. Your value does not diminish because you are alone. On the contrary, you lose value if you have been everywhere with everyone.

C. I am the chooser, not just the chosen

Proverbs 12:26 says, *"The righteous should chose his friends carefully."* When you go to a store, you pick up an item or a commodity from the shelf or the rack, you take it to the counter; you pay for it and take it home. The item does not have a say whatsoever in the decision of whether to go with you or not. In preparing for marriage, if you are not a bag, a shoe, or a car, you must have a say in the issue. If someone says to you, 'I choose you,' you can either say 'I choose you too,' or 'I don't choose you.' If anyone comes and says, 'God said to me that you are my wife/husband,' tell him/her to also allow God to speak to you too, considering that you are half of the equation. Don't be carried away by that classic statement, 'GOD TOLD ME.'

I have a personal experience when I was the youth president many years ago in a Christian organisation, where three brothers approached a particular sister in my group that God them that she was their future partner. The sister was so confused, primarily because the so-called suitors were 'spiritual' brothers and she confided in me as her president. Of course, I confronted the three brothers; first individually to verify their stories, and when they each maintained their tales, I arranged a meeting with them together. They were so embarrassed of themselves when their deceit was exposed. In the final analysis, none of them married the lady, who is now happily married to someone else. As a rule, always first decide prayerfully and realistically the qualities you want in a spouse, and when someone comes along and meets them, then you will know.

D. I look and listen before I leap

Luke 14:28-30 says, *"For which of you, intending to build a tower, does not sit down first and count the cost, whether he has enough to finish it lest, after he has laid the foundation and is not able to finish, all who see it begin to mock him, saying this man began to build and was no able to finish."*

Love, they say, is blind, but marriage is an eye-opener. Research has shown that most problems that manifest in marriage were already there during courtship, but they were ignored. People believe that after marriage, something is going to miraculously happen that will put things right. Please, young people, open your eyes before you say 'I do'. Get over those superficial, flimsy, physical attractions. Consider their mannerisms. Proverbs 31:30 says, *"Charm is deceitful and beauty is passing, but the woman that fears the Lord she shall be praised."* Watch their manners, not towards you only, but towards other people they are not trying to impress.

Consider things like:
- How does he/she behave to people below him/her?
- How loyal is he/she to his/her friends?
- How readily does he/she accept responsibilities for his/her actions?
- How quickly does he/she apologise for his/her mistakes?
- How does he/she treat his/her enemies?
- How respectful is he/she to his/her parents?
- Does he/she always keep his/her promises?
- How genuinely does he/she love God and serve him?

As you prepare to cross the road from singleness to marriage, stop, look and listen before you leap.

CONCLUSION

The preparation for your marital future is of utmost importance and it cannot wait. Having made the choice to marry, the time to start working on how your future home is going to look is now. Be aware that the responsibility of choosing a partner is yours. It is too important to leave in the hands of anyone, neither should you leave it to chance.

Proverbs 18:22 says, *"He who finds a wife finds a good thing and obtains favour from the Lord."*(NKJV). Someone once said that since the fall of man in the Garden of Eden, where Adam blamed his disobedience on the wife God gave him, God has passed the duty of finding a wife to the man so that there will be no more avoidance of attendant consequences of our choices. Let the spirit of God guide you. Prayerfully begin to ask God to direct your path and lead you to the right person for your life. Someone that will compliment and better your life. The person who is going the same way as you Amos 3:3 says, *"Can two work together, unless they are agreed?"* Seek for the one who has the fear of God in his/her heart. The bible says in Proverbs 1:7, *"The fear of the Lord is the beginning of knowledge, but fools despise wisdom and instruction."*

It is the fear of the Lord that keeps a man and a woman faithful in marriage. It is the fear of the Lord that makes a man take up his roles and responsibilities in a marriage. Apostle Paul, writing to the young Timothy said in 1 Timothy 5:8, *"But if any provide not for his own, and especially for those of his own house, he hath denied the faith and is worse than an infidel."* (KJV). It is the fear of God that makes a woman acknowledge her roles in the family without feeling insecure. Proverbs 14:1 says, *"The wise woman builds her house, but the foolish pulls it down with her hands."* (NKJV). It is the fear of God that produces the wisdom to train children and the next generation in the way of the Lord. Proverbs 22:6 says, *"Train up a child in the way he should go and when he is old he will not depart from it."*

> ***It is the fear of the Lord that keeps a man and a woman faithful in marriage.***

I decree and declare by the power and the spirit of the Lord, that the spirit of wisdom to choose rightly be released upon you as you read this book in Jesus' name. The grace not to make a mistake in regards to marriage be available unto you now. The power to discern by the spirit of God every deceit of the enemy to confuse you in your choice of a life partner be released upon you now in Jesus' name. The anointing to enjoy and not endure your marriage will be given unto you now. You shall not fail, you shall not falter, you shall not miss the mark in marriage in Jesus' name.

I proclaim that your marriage shall be exemplary for others to copy. May your marriage challenge and encourage the next generation to godly living. May you leave a legacy of good marriage and a model of a Christian home. Every attack of the devil on your preparation for marriage is cursed in Jesus' name. I thwart and destroy every attempt of the devil to destroy your marriage in Jesus' name. The Lord will give you divine insight and understanding to plan, choose a partner, and enjoy your marriage in Jesus' name.

God bless you.

See you at the top!

CHAPTER 5

A CALL TO ACTION

Having looked at the four major areas of preparation for tomorrow in the previous chapters, it is pertinent to understand that God has ordained and chosen you from the foundation of the world to be His own. He loves you with an everlasting love that is not dependent on what you do or do not do. His love for you knows no bound and it was demonstrated on the cross of Calvary when Jesus laid his life down for you.

You can read this book and think that it is fantastic and you desire everything great therein. But you need to understand that actions need to accomplish your desire if it is ever going to materialise. There are steps you need to take to secure a better and glorious tomorrow for yourself and generations after. Only you can determine whether you are hungry enough for the changes that need to happen. Someone once said,, 'There are three types of people in the world. Firstly, there are people who make things happen. Then there are people who watch things happen. Lastly, there are people who ask, what happened? Which do you want to be?'

> *There are steps you need to take to secure a better and glorious tomorrow for yourself and generations after.*

I encourage you today to look at these following foundational truths that will help you achieve a brighter tomorrow;

Truth No.1: Remember Your Creator Now Solomon in Ecclesiastes 12:1-7 (NLT), *"Don't let the excitement of youth cause you to forget your Creator. Honor him in your youth before you grow old and say, "Life is not pleasant anymore." 2 Remember him before the light of the sun, moon, and stars is dim to your old eyes, and rain clouds continually darken your sky. 3 Remember him before your legs—the guards of your house—start to tremble; and before your shoulders—the strong men—stoop. Remember him before your teeth—your few remaining servants—stop grinding; and before your eyes—the women looking through the windows—see dimly. 4 Remember him before the door to life's opportunities is closed and the sound of work fades. Now you rise at the first chirping of the birds, but then all their sounds will grow faint.*

5 Remember him before you become fearful of falling and worry about danger in the streets; before your hair turns white like an almond tree in bloom, and you drag along without energy like a dying grasshopper, and the caperberry no longer inspires sexual desire. Remember him before you near the grave, your everlasting home, when the mourners will weep at your funeral. 6 Yes, remember your Creator now while you are young, before the silver cord of life snaps and the golden bowl is broken. Don't wait until the water jar is smashed at the spring and the pulley is broken at the well. 7 For then the dust will return to the earth, and the spirit will return to God who gave it."

The first and most important step in life for anyone who wants to have a glorious tomorrow is to remember his/her creator now. A life without God will definitely end in bitterness and hopelessness in old age. You cannot escape God throughout your life. You will either serve him willingly now or be forced to bow in judgement before Him later. Choose wisely today. I was watching the funeral of Whitney Houston the other day and I was so sad when her lifeless body was brought into the same church, where she began her singing career in the choir at the age of eleven, before she completely lost her way and died of drug addiction and overdose.

Being young is exciting and that excitement can, if not properly channelled, lead us away from God, by focussing our attention on temporal, fleeting and passing pleasures of life, instead on eternal values. A wise counsellor once gave me this advice when I was younger and without direction in life, 'Make your strength and vigour available to God now that you are young. A time is coming when you will want to do the things you can do now, but the strength will no longer be there'. How true. For instance, I used to be a very good footballer in my younger days. I could play for hours on end and days none stop. Some months back, my church organised a sports day for men and we were asked to play some football matches. You don't want to know what happened before, during and days after the event.

Secondly, reverence and serve God with the whole of your life. V. 13-14 of the same Ecclesiastes 12 says, *"That's the whole story. Here now is my final conclusion: Fear God and obey his commands, for this is everyone's duty. 14 God will judge us for everything we do, including every secret thing, whether good or bad."* (NLT).

Please know that serving God is not just for the elderly. Great men and women of God served Him from their youth. People like Joseph, Samuel, David, Daniel in the bible and…. In our days. Add your name to that list. The benefit of serving God from your youth is that it will help you make the right choices. Look at Joseph in Genesis 39:7-12, where he was being offered and pressured to have free sex with his master's wife, *"And Potiphar's wife soon began to look at him lustfully. "Come and sleep with me," she demanded. 8 But Joseph refused. "Look," he told her, "my master trusts me with everything in his entire household. 9 No one here has more authority than I do. He has held back nothing from me except you, because you are his wife. How could I do such a wicked thing? It would be a great sin against God." 10 She kept putting pressure on Joseph day after day, but he refused to sleep with her, and he kept out of her way as much as possible. 11 One day, however, no one else was around when he went in to do his work. 12 She came and grabbed him by his cloak, demanding, "Come on, sleep with me!" Joseph tore himself away, but he left his cloak in her hand as he ran from the house."* (NLT).

Another example of that is Daniel in the land of Babylon. He was a young man in slavery but in spite of his situation, in Daniel 1:8. *"But Daniel was determined not to defile himself by eating the food and wine given to them by the king. He asked the chief of staff for permission not to eat these unacceptable foods."* (NLT).

As you plan for tomorrow, remember to serve God in your youth, being assured of the fact that God is going to reward you abundantly. Paul said in Galatians 6:7-9, *"Do not be deceived, God is not mocked; for whatever a man sows, that he will also reap. For he who sows to his flesh will of the flesh reap corruption, but he who sows to the Spirit will of the Spirit reap everlasting life. And let us not grow weary while doing good, for in due season we shall reap if we do not lose heart."*

The above action steps are a natural by products of discovering our purpose as explained in the first chapter which is the essence of our spiritual preparation.

Chapters 2 to 4 talks about Educational, Financial and Marital preparation in which we are encouraged to take practical and measurable steps to get ourselves ready for the future. Please note that as you lay your bed, so you lie on it. Irrespective of where you are today, you can decide to take action to better your life. You must be ready however to pay the price. No pain, no gain. It will be half - truth to say that once you pray, all your problems are solved. You need to acquire the prerequisite wisdom necessary to navigate the course of life. You need to acquire knowledge, seek understanding and obtain wisdom. There is a difference between these words.

Knowledge is the accumulation of facts or information through experience or education. Understanding is the mental grasp or comprehension of those facts and information, while Wisdom is the right application of those facts and information gained. Wisdom is the principal thing, the bible says. Education, as good and useful as it is, needs to be rightly applied to be of any benefit to you and the society at large.

Wisdom is acquired through thinking. This is not only true in spiritual things, but all across other aspects of life. *"As a man thinketh in his heart, so is he."* A man is literally what he thinks, his character being the complete sum of all his thoughts. Whatever level you are today is a direct result of your thoughts. If you think you can achieve success and a better tomorrow, you can, and if you think you can't, then you wouldn't. You must change your thought pattern to such that can see possibilities in every adversity. You need to understand that a bend in the road is not the end of the road. There is always light at the end of the tunnel. Determine to better your academic lot. Start by setting reasonable and achievable targets to improve your lot. Let every year take you closer to that goal. I have always wanted to be a lawyer, because I found out early in life that I love helping people especially the less privileged. I hate injustice and I love to better people's lot. I have been involved in Students' Unionism at various stages, levels and capacities and when I started working in a very big company, I just got involved in the Labour movement which afforded me the opportunity to help quite a lot of people.

All of that prompted me, when I relocated to the UK to enrol in a University to study Law. Even though I am not fully practicing as a lawyer, you cannot imagine, by the grace of God, how many destinies have been affected by that decision. What is your passion? What would you like to be known for? Start out today to pursue that goal. A journey of a thousand miles, they say begins with a step in the right direction. Get up and start where you are. You can never know how far you will go until you start. There is something on the inside of you that the next generation is waiting for. Do not let it die with you. My birthday is always a very emotional period for me because I receive messages from young men and women scattered all over the world who send wishes and remind me of how I have positively influenced their lives while growing up. It gives me a sense of fulfilment that no amount of money can buy and I am always grateful to God for that grace. The key here is to never stop learning. Always aspire for the next level. Someone said 'if you cannot fly, then run, if you cannot run, then walk, if you cannot walk, then crawl, but by all means, keep moving'

> *You can never know how far you will go until you start.*

On the topic of financial preparation, start on the journey to financial independence now. Ask God to give you divine ideas that will translate into financial breakthroughs. Remember you can pray until you are blue in the face, if you do not follow the principles of financial breakthrough, you will remain poor forever. Those principles answer to you whether you are a Christian or not. I have met some great spiritual people in my time who are poor. It is not because God cannot bless them or they have no need for finance, it's just that they lack the required knowledge of the principles they need to follow. 2 Kings 4:1 says, *"Now there cried a certain woman of the wives of the sons of the prophets unto Elisha, saying, Thy servant my husband is dead; and thou knowest that thy servant did fear the Lord: and the creditor is come to take unto him my two sons to be bondmen."* (KJV). I challenge you to find out from the scriptures those timeless principles. When people like Bishop David Oyedepo make such pronouncements like 'I can never be poor', please find out where they are coming from. What do they know that needs to be learnt. I used to accuse him of spiritual arrogance, until I discovered that, he only searched the scripture to discover the principles of financial prosperity. You can love him or hate him, but you can never argue against his results. Some of the principles are what we have highlighted in chapter 3 earlier.

Reading this book and just commending it will do you no good. The action steps need to be taken. I crave you indulgence to obey those principles. Just like hearing a good message without doing anything about it will do no one any good, so also reading a good book without practising the principles laid down there will not do you any good. James 1:22-25 says, *"But be doers of the word, and not hearers only, deceiving yourselves. For if anyone is a hearer of the word and not a doer, he is like a man observing his natural face in a mirror; for he observes himself, goes away, and immediately forgets what kind of man he was. But he who looks into the perfect law of liberty and continues in it, and is not a forgetful hearer but a doer of the work, this one will be blessed in what he does."*

Finally, in relation to marital preparation, I will want to emphasise that building a family is like building a house, and like every good house that is built on a solid foundation can and will withstand the inevitable storms. Every marriage built on a solid foundation will also withstand every storm that rises against it. The familiar story of two men who built their houses as told by Jesus in Matthew 27:24-27, *"Therefore whoever hears these sayings of Mine, and does them, I will liken him to a wise man who built his house on the rock: and the rain descended, the floods came, and the winds blew and beat on that house; and it did not fall, for it was founded on the rock. "But everyone who hears these sayings of Mine, and does not do them, will be like a foolish man who built his house on the sand: and the rain descended, the floods came, and the winds blew and beat on that house; and it fell. And great was its fall."*

The same passage from the message version of the bible reads (MSG), *"These words I speak to you are not incidental additions to your life, homeowner improvements to your standard of living. They are foundational words, words to build a life on. If you work these words into your life, you are like a smart carpenter who built his house on solid rock. ". Rain poured down, the river flooded, a tornado hit—but nothing moved that house. It was fixed to the rock. "But if you just use my words in Bible studies and don't work them into your life, you are like a stupid carpenter who built his house on the sandy beach. When a storm rolled in and the waves came up, it collapsed like a house of cards."*

70

A storm can be defined as a violent and adverse weather condition. It can also be defined as a sudden attack on a secure position.

For every marriage to stand the test of time, the following truths have to be known and the principles applied;

1. Good homes or marital futures do not just happen, they are planned for and carefully built.

Take charge of your marital future now. Begin by praying for your future partner now. Tell God to make it impossible for you to make a mistake in the choice of a life partner. That was one of my prayer items years before I got married.

2. A good home just like a good house must be built for strength and not just beauty.

Look out for good qualities in your future partner, not just the external flimsy attributes. 2 Corinthians 4:18 says, *"While we do not look at the things which are seen, but at the things which are not seen. For the things which are seen are temporary, but the things which are not seen are eternal."* Proverbs 31:30 says, *"Charm is deceitful and beauty is passing, but a woman who fears the Lord, she shall be praised."*

In as much as beauty is right, you need to look for strength of character, strong moral convictions and the fear of God in a future partner. What is the use of a beautiful house that will collapse in the face of the slightest wind.

3. Every family, just like every house, will experience a storm.

Life operates in seasons and every season brings its own peculiar kind of weather with it. Your family will be tested and issues will come against you in such a way that is not expected. There is no amount of prayer that can prevent storms from coming. Jesus said in John 16:33, *"These things I have spoken to you, that in Me you may have peace. In the world you will[a] have tribulation; but be of good cheer, I have overcome the world."*

4. Just like the wise man in Jesus' parable, always build with the storm in mind.

Hope for the good days, but build for the bad days. The concept of Insurance illustrates this aptly. When you take up insurance on your house, car and other valuables, you never pray that you use them. But inevitably, you might need to use them. If they are not there, it results into serious pressure and avoidable troubles. Towards the end of 2013, I was involved in a car accident in which my car was written off by the insurer. Within hours of the incident, a replacement car was arranged until they could settle the claim, which was sorted out within a week. Imagine if there was no insurance in place. I also know a neighbour of mine who had no insurance on their property, unfortunately there was a serious fire which gulfed the whole house. As at the time of writing this book, which is over a year now, the house still lies in ruin.

5. Lastly, always remember that the strength of every family, just like a house begins with the foundation.

Psalm 11:15 says, *"If the foundations are destroyed, What can the righteous do?"* Lay a solid foundation for your future home. Deliberately decide to obey God, the originator of marriage, in preparing for you future. Don't cut corners. Flee sexual immorality as a young person. Keep yourself pure and wait for God's leading in this all important choice.

At the start of this chapter, I briefly talked about the grace and love of God that is available to everyone and the unconditionality of that love. This is even more true in regards to people who have erred and missed the mark at some point in life. You may be reading this book and say that, 'Well, I am a teenage girl with a child already, or I am an ex-convict even at a young age'. Let me say to you that, there is hope for you. You can pick up the pieces of that shattered life and make something beautiful out of your it.

The God that we serve is a God of many chances. He pardons and forgives and He gives new life. He is not interested in the death of any sinner, rather He gives the opportunity for a fresh start. He said in Isaiah 1:18, *"Come now, and let us reason together, says the LORD: though your sins be as scarlet, they shall be as white as snow; though they be red like crimson, they shall be as wool."*

You can consider the lives of people like Joseph, who was sold into slavery because of his dreams of a better tomorrow, by his brothers. He got into Egypt as a slave, worked as a houseboy, was thrown into prison for what he did not do, but in all these situations, he held on to God and his dreams. God eventually took him from the dungeon and he became the prime minister in a foreign land. Genesis 41:39-44, *"39 Then Pharaoh said to Joseph, "Inasmuch as God has shown you all this, there is no one as discerning and wise as you. 40 You shall be over my house, and all my people shall be ruled according to your word; only in regard to the throne will I be greater than you." 41 And Pharaoh said to Joseph, "See, I have set you over all the land of Egypt". 42 Then Pharaoh took his signet ring off his hand and put it on Joseph's hand; and he clothed him in garments of fine linen and put a gold chain around his neck. 43 And he had him ride in the second chariot which he had; and they cried out before him, "Bow the knee!" So he set him over all the land of Egypt. 44 Pharaoh also said to Joseph, "I am Pharaoh, and without your consent no man may lift his hand or foot in all the land of Egypt."*

He could have lost hope, stopped serving God. He could have sat down and be despondent all his life. He had enough reasons to not achieve his potentials and blame it on the hatred he experienced from his brothers. But he didn't, he did not allow his past to hold him down. He achieved his destiny. I proclaim by the power in the name of Jesus that you will achieve your destiny. No matter what your past is, there is hope in your tomorrow. If a young Hebrew slave boy could rise to become the second in command in Egypt, then your story must and will end well in Jesus name.

Another young man who found himself in a precarious situation was Daniel. His land had been raided, the people including himself taken captive by a foreign super power, because of the sins of his leaders. He found himself, at a very young age in Babylon with all the attractions to sins and vices, which he had to resist on a daily basis. First was the refusal to eat of the king's delicacies, which had the possibility of defiling him before God. Daniel 1:8, *"But Daniel purposes in his heart that he would not defile himself with the portion of the king's delicacies, nor with the wine which he drank; therefore he requested of the chief of the eunuchs that he might not defile himself."* Daniel also had more than enough reasons to let go his God given destiny and blame everyone for his captivity and slavery, but he chose to focus on the greater tomorrow and for a period spanning over 70 years, he served four different regimes in various capacities.

The life of Oprah Winfrey is a case study of how we should not allow our start in life, our ugly pasts and the many adversities we face in life to deter us from achieving a better tomorrow for ourselves. It shows and proves to us that you can achieve your potentials and become all that God has created you to become if only you will not sit back and wallow in self-pity.

Oprah Gail Winfrey (born January 29, 1954) is an American media proprietor, talk show host, actress, producer, and philanthropist. Born to an unwed teenage mother, Oprah Winfrey spent her first years on her grandmother's farm in Kosciusko, Mississippi, while her mother looked for work in the North. Life on the farm was primitive, but her grandmother taught her to read at an early age, and at age three Oprah was reciting poems and Bible verses in local churches. Despite the hardships of her physical environment, she enjoyed the loving support of her grandmother and the church community, who cherished her as a gifted child. Her world changed for the worse at age six, when she was sent to Milwaukee to live with her mother, who had found work as a housemaid. In the long days when her mother was absent from their inner city apartment, young Oprah was repeatedly molested by male relatives and another visitor. The abuse, which lasted from the ages of nine to 13, was emotionally devastating. When she tried to run away, she was sent to a juvenile detention home, only to be denied admission because all the beds were filled. At 14, she was out of the house and on her own. By her own account, she was sexually promiscuous as a teenager. After giving birth to a baby boy who died in infancy, she went to Nashville, Tennessee to live with her father.

Winfrey is best known for her multi- award winning talk show, The Oprah Winfrey Show, which was the highest-rated program of its kind in history and was nationally syndicated from 1986 to 2011. Dubbed the "Queen of All Media", she has been ranked the richest African-American of the 20th century, the greatest black philanthropist in American history, and is currently North America's only black billionaire. She is also, according to some assessments, the most influential woman in the world. In 2013, she was awarded the Presidential Medal of Freedom by President Barack Obama and an honorary doctorate degree from Harvard University.

Today, Oprah Winfrey makes her principal home on a 42-acre ocean-view estate in Montecito, California, just south of Santa Barbara, but also owns homes in other six states and the island of Antigua. The business press measures her wealth in numerous superlatives: the highest-paid performer on television, the richest self-made woman in America, and the richest African-American of the 20th century. More difficult to calculate is her profound influence over the way people around the world read, eat, exercise, feel and think about themselves and the world around them. She appears on every list of the world's leading opinion-makers, and has been rightly called 'the most powerful woman in the world.'

Her wide-ranging philanthropic efforts were recognized by the Academy of Motion Picture Arts and Sciences in 2011 with a special Oscar statuette, the Jean Hersholt Humanitarian Award - (sources: The free Wikipedia, Oprah Winfrey, Academy of achievement, Biography of Oprah Winfrey, America's Beloved Best Friend).

She was quoted to have said, 'It doesn't matter who you are, where you come from. The ability to triumph begins with you. Always.' And I dare add that, that ability is already on the inside of you, given to you by your creator before you were even conceived and birthed. Rise up and discover that ability. Ask God to help you use it and make your tomorrow glorious and enviable. These are the action steps required in your quest for a better tomorrow. When you take these practical steps, you will, by the help of the most high God guarantee your future.

See you at the top!

CLOSING PRAYER

FOR TOMORROW

I will end this book by encouraging you to sincerely pray these powerful prophetic prayers into your life. Remember, it is your sole duty to deliver yourself from every limiting and militating factors that you may be facing or will be facing in your tomorrow.

Ask God to reveal His purpose for your existence to you NOW.

Pray that nothing will take the place of God Almighty in your life.

Ask God to restore back to you the dominion mandate he gave you in Genesis 1:26-27.

Ask God to reveal yourself to you.

Ask the Holy Spirit of God to purify your heart.

Make my life count for something worthwhile oh Lord.

Change my story for good.

Help me to finish my course on earth well.

Let me not disappoint destinies that are tied to mine.

I refuse to be a failure in life.

Grant me the grace to serve you whole heartedly

Fortify me against all attacks of the devil.

Ask God to give you the power and the wisdom to create wealth.

Ask God to make it impossible for you to make a mistake in the choice of a life partner.

Make my marriage a good example for others oh Lord.

Ask God to help you build your home on a solid foundation of His word.

May I pronounce, by the spirit of the Lord on you, that God Almighty bless you and make His face shine on you. May He grant you peace and make your name great. May generations yet unborn call you blessed. I declare that your name will be mentioned in high places. You will seat with kings and princes. The grace of the lord in your life will announce your name before celebrities and lift you up. The height that no one in your family has ever reached, you will reach and surpass in Jesus' name. As you determine to serve the Lord, you will not lose your place in life. As you walk in reverence of the Lord, may your path in life be brighten up continually. You will excel in all the work of your hands. I declare that your eye of understanding be opened more and more. The grace of God locate and single you out for blessing. As you obey the words of the Lord, I decree wisdom that is above your age and your contemporaries be released on your life. You will never lack divine direction all the days of your life. Innovations that will change lives and perpetuate blessings for your generation be released to you now. Where God has destined for you to reach, you will get there. Sin, satan and self will not stop you. It is well with you in Jesus mighty name I pray.

A PRAYER OF SALVATION

Dear friend, the greatest and most important preparation you can make is the one for eternity. Let me ask you these simple questions?

Have you at any time given your life to Jesus Christ? Are you sure that if you died today, you will spend eternity with God in heaven? Are you definite that your name is written in the book of Life? Are you filled with the Holy Spirit of God?

If you cannot answer YES to any of the above questions with assurance, I will like to lead you in a short prayer. Please say this with me; 'Lord Jesus, I come to you today. I recognise that I need you in my life. I come just as I am with my load of sins. Have mercy on me. Wash me with your precious blood. I denounce and reject Satan and all his ways. I accept you Lord Jesus into my life. Come and be my master and friend from today. Write my name in the book of life. Help me through my journey in life. Direct me by your Holy Spirit. Thank you Lord for accepting me into your family, in Jesus name I pray"

I want to say a big congratulation to you for taking the most important step in your preparation towards your eternity. For further help in this new decision of yours, feel free to reach me on

WHAT ABOUT TOMORROW?

femilawani05@yahoo.co.uk. Join me on my Facebook page Olufemi Lawani and on twitter #whatabouttomorrow.

See you at the top!